Pytorch Deep Learning by Example, Vol.1 (3rd Edition)

Contents

List of Figures

List of Tables

Do you have difficulties to even get started on pytorch?
Do you have trouble to really understand pytorch example code?
Do you want to understand many state-of-art deep learning technologies with bare-minimum math?
Do you have obstacles to implement a real life deep learning projects in pytorch?

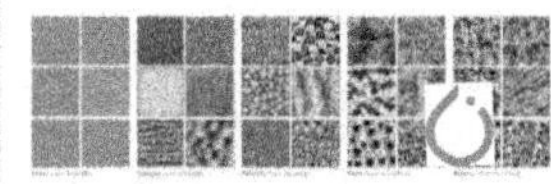

This book series will easy these pains and help you learn and grasp deep learning technology from ground zero with many i
nteresting real world examples implemented in pytorch.

In this book series, you will learn:

* a basic deep learning concepts/theory with bare-minimum math
* a deep-dived/well-explained MNIST CNN example so that you can really understand pytorch model, how to choose los
s, optimizer in pytorch etc.
* how to use a pre-trained model by using transfer learning/fine-tune techniques.
* what are CNN, RNN, Seq2Seq,word embedding, CTC, Auto-encoder, DMN, DQN/DDQN,MCTS,Alphago/Alphazero etc, and how
they work.
* How those deep learning technologies are applied to NLP, OCR, Speech, Computer Games etc.

This is Volume 1.

Pytorch Deep Learning by Example Vol. 1

Benjamin Young

Pytorch Deep Learning by Example Vol. 1

Fundamentals - Grasp deep Learning from scratch like AlphaGo Zero within 40 days(3rd Edition)

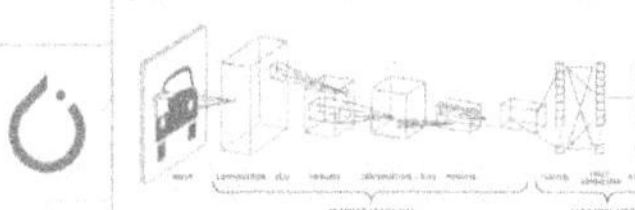

PyTorch

Benjamin Young

Copyright

For permission requests, email to author, at the address below:

benjamin@comrite.com

Web URL: http://www.comrite.com

Preface

Artificial Intelligence (AI) could be traced back to the 1950s. It went through several hype/bust cycles. In 2010, we entered the era of AI, this time deep learning (a branch of AI) took a leading role.

Over the past years, deep learning has gone from a niche field comprised of a few researchers to being sort of mainstream. It made incredibly progress in many areas, such as: image classification, voice recognition, text generation, language translation etc.

As time goes by, it became apparent that deep learning would stay in the mainstream.

As a technology person, it is time to keep updated with these new skill sets.

Well, to really understand deep learning, a deep dive into math is normally needed.

Fortunately, tech world/knowledge are normally built on layers/blocks. Researchers/scientists have built a great deep learning foundation for us, we will stand on the shoulders of giants. In this book we will mainly focus on applications on top of them. From practical engineering point of view, We may not need a deep dive into math in order to use it effectively. Just like we can write an awesome software running on CPU, we generally do not need to have a very deep understanding of CPU.

So in this book, we are not trying to deep dive into the math, instead we are trying to get an intuition of neural network, understand deep learning deep enough so that we could use and apply it effectively in our daily job/use cases.

I hope this book could help others who do not have a formal deep learning/AI course/training to learn deep learning quickly.

Example source code could be found at:

https://github.com/mingewang/pytorch_deep_learning_by_example

Remember, being a relatively new technology, deep learning is not perfect. It requires an investment of both time and money, as well as the expertise to use it, not just for the researcher, but for the programmer too.

I welcome emails from any readers with comments, suggestions, or bug fixes.

Benjamin Young

benjamin@comrite.com

Aug, 2019

About Volume I/II

Volume I is focused on deep learning, and pytorch fundamentals.

Volume II is focused on advanced applications.

Disclaimer

Although the author and publisher have made every effort to ensure that the information in this book was correct at press time, the author and publisher do not assume and hereby disclaim any liability to any party for any loss, damage, or disruption caused by errors or omissions, whether such errors or omissions result from negligence, accident, or any other cause.

Acknowledgments

I would like to thank the invaluable support from my family for their patience while I worked late, often and sometimes on vacation.

Chapter 1

Introduction

Quote from Wikipedia:

Deep learning (DL) (also known as deep structured learning or hierarchical learning) is part of a broader family of machine learning methods based on learning data representations, as opposed to task-specific algorithms. Learning can be supervised, semi-supervised or unsupervised.

It is a class of machine learning algorithms that **uses multiple layers to progressively extract higher level features from the raw input**.

Deep-learning is one of the most exciting areas nowadays.

With deep-learning

- self-driving cars can to detect/see (computer vision) cars, people nearby.
- voice recognition dramatically improved the error rate by using deep-learning. e.g: google's speech to text can reach 4.9% word error rate at the time of writing. Amazon's echo, google now, Apple's siri, etc are those voice search and voice assistant application.
- Modern computers have started to recognize many objects from images, video streams. Those technologies can be used in many areas, e.g: medical, security, etc.
- The accuracy of machine translations improved dramatically. Google's translation system was reported approaching human-level accuracy.

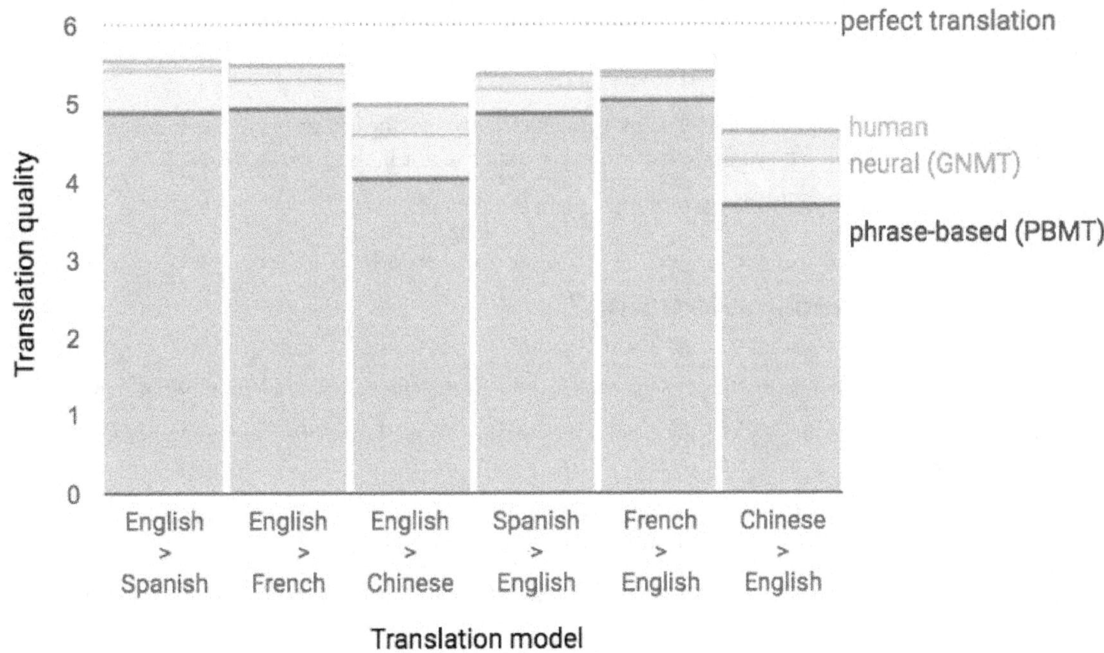

Figure 1.1: google translation quality

- Handwriting recognition has been improved greatly (the same as voice recognition)
- Face-detection now reaches a much higher accuracy rate ever.
- Colorization of Black and White Images is possible.
- Advertising has been transformed to increase the relevancy of publisher's ads and boost the return on investment of their advertising campaigns.
- Character Text Generation.
- Image Caption Generation.
- Automatic Game Playing.

...

The list could go on and on ...

Quote from Andrew Ng, a famous AI researcher:

"AI is the new electricity. About 100 years ago, electricity transformed every major industry. AI has advanced to the point where it has the power to transform every major sector in the coming years. "

Deep learning will definitely play a very big role in the AI world.

1.1 what is machine learning?

Before we dive into deep learning, let's go back a little bit to get a better understanding of machine learning.

The term "machine learning" (ML) was coined by Arthur Samuel (an American computer gaming/AI pioneer) in 1959 while at IBM.

More precisely, ML tries to build a mathematical model of sample data/training data, in order to make predictions or decisions without being explicitly programmed to perform the task.

Acute readers may notice that ML differs dramatically from our familiar/traditional programming model.

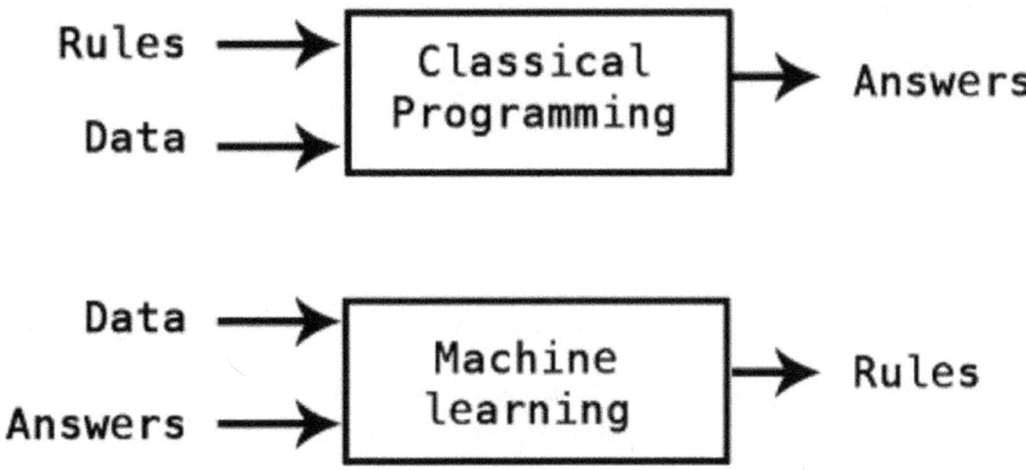

Figure 1.2: machine learning is different from classical programming

The figure above shows the difference clearly.

For classical programming, we build software with rules or prior knowledge etc to process data, then get answers.

While in machine learning, we feed data and answers into the ML system, we let the ML system find the rules for us. That sounds magical, right?

Stay tuned, one purpose of this book is to decipher this magic.

Tip
What is the difference between ML and data mining? ML focuses on prediction based on known properties learned from the training data, while data mining focuses on the discovery of (previously) unknown properties in the data.

1.2 machine learning types

Machine learning are generally categorized as: supervised, unsupervised, self-supervised, reinforcement learning, etc. Different learning types will use different strategies/algorithms.

1.2.1 supervised learning

Supervised learning's goal is to learn a function that, given a sample of data and desired outputs, best approximates the relationship between input and output observable in the data.

In another word, it tries to find some interesting transformations of the input data with the help of target/ground truth.

The learning algorithm makes predictions on the training data, corrects itself by comparing the prediction with the associated target/ground truth. The process will continues iteratively until the difference between prediction and ground true are within an acceptable level.

Supervised learning can be further grouped into:

- **classification** problems: when we want to map an input to output labels
- **regression** problems: when we want to map an input to continuous output.

Tip

what is label? We sometimes call target or ground truth as label.

Almost all applications of deep learning that are in the spotlight these days belong to this category, for example: optical character recognition, speech recognition, image classification, and language translation etc.

1.2.2 unsupervised learning

Unsupervised learning is very useful in the exploratory analysis because it can automatically identify structure in data.

It consists of finding interesting transformations of the input data without the help of any targets/ground truth facts.

The most common tasks in this category are clustering, representation learning, and density estimation etc.

Other tasks in unsupervised learning area are quite challenging.

As you can imagine, unsupervised learning is not as mature as supervised learning.

1.2.3 self-supervised learning

Self-supervised learning can be viewed as a special kind of supervised learning, but without human-annotated labels, in another word, labels are generated from the input data, typically using a heuristic algorithm etc.

The autoencoder is a such great example.

1.2.4 reinforcement learning RL

Reinforcement learning is somehow between supervised learning and unsupervised learning.

In RL, there are several components: agent, environment, and reward. The agent will receive information about its environment, learns to choose actions that will maximize the reward.

For instance, a neural network can "look" at a video-game screen, and try to learn which game action can maximize its score.

Currently, RL is mostly a research area and has not yet had significant practical successes beyond games.

We will learn some reinforcement learning algorithms in this book.

1.3 A little bit of history about deep learning.

The concept of neural network dates back to the 1940-50s.

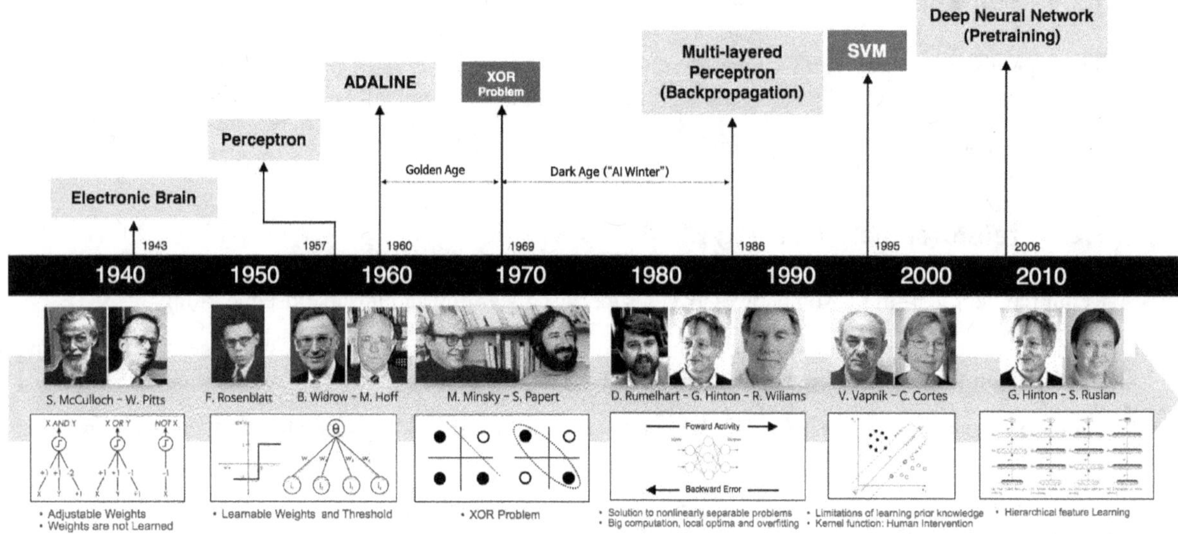

Figure 1.3: history diagram of deep learning

In 1943, Warren McCulloch and Walter Pitts created a computational model for neural networks based on mathematics, and algorithms called threshold logic.

Around the 1970s, the research of neural network slowed down after Minsky and Papert's paper (1969), which claimed that computers at that time didn't have enough processing power to handle the work required by large neural networks.

In 1975, Werbos invented a backpropagation algorithm, which laid the foundation of today's deep learning neural network.

Around 1980-1990, many other key ML algorithms were discovered.

In 1986, Rina Dechter (a female computer profession at UC, Irvine) introduced the term **Deep Learning**.

Around 2006, Hinton (from University of Toronto), etc. proposed a many-layer feed-forward neural network, which spiked the "deep learning" wave.

In 2012, Alex Krizhevsky, Ilya Sutskever, and Geoff Hinton proposed an **Alexnet**, which reduced the error rate to a breakthrough low 16% for Large Scale Visual Recognition Challenge(LSVRC).

It is believed that Alexnet marked the start of an industry-wide artificial intelligence boom.

In 2017, many research teams got less than 5% for LSVRC.

1.4 Why deep learning now?

Many core concepts for deep learning were in place by the 80s or 90s, why did we make leap-frog improvements only recently (around the 2010s)?

There are many contributing factors, two most crucial components are:

(1) availability of massive data (labeled data sets)

Massive labeled data make it possible to train a deep neural network model to low error rate without losing its generality.

One famous free dataset is ImageNet, which is a large visual database designed for use in visual object recognition. It has more than 14 million hand-annotated images, 20,000 categories.

The recent trend showed that accessibility of massive high quality data will continue.

Many datasets could be found here:

https://en.wikipedia.org/wiki/List_of_datasets_for_machine_learning_research

(2) massive amount of computational power.

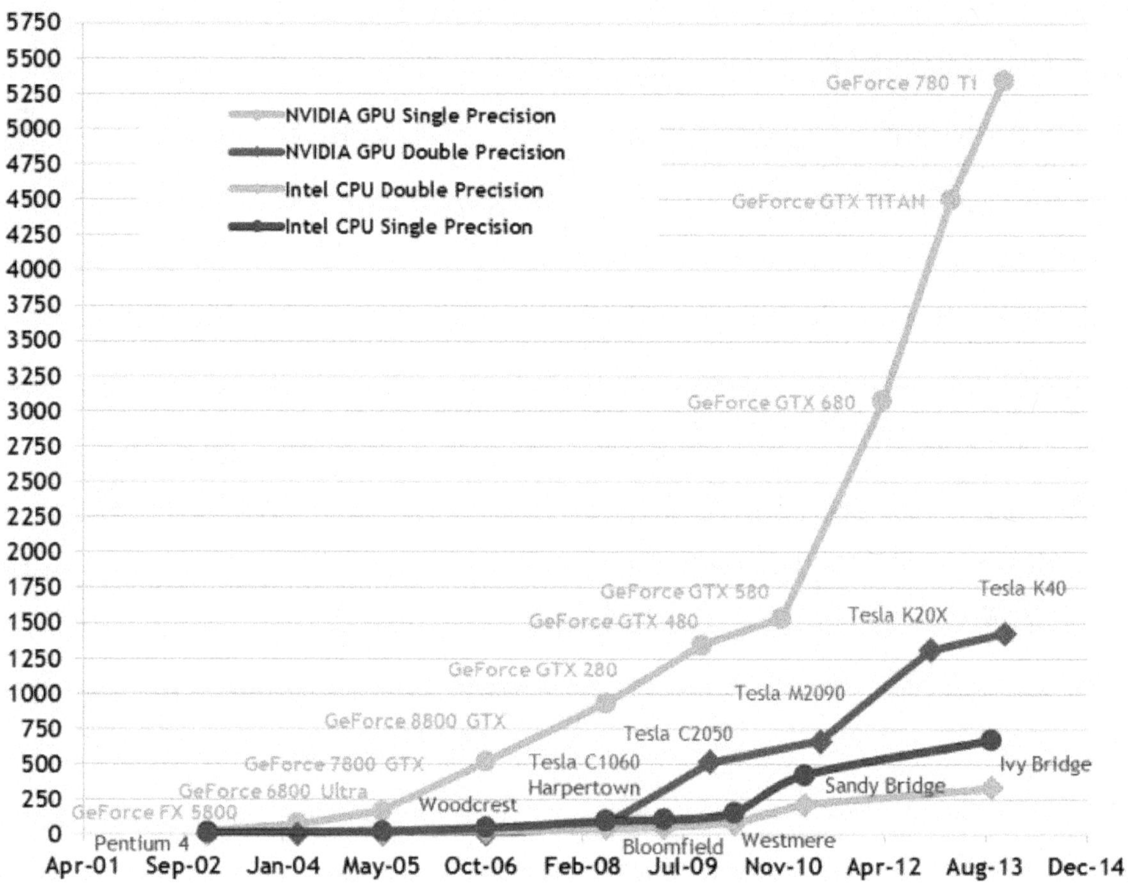

Figure 1.4: GPU computing power from NVIDIA Cuda C Programming Guide.

Graphics Processing Units (GPUs) uses a powerful parallel programming model, provides a massive computing power.

Hundred-cores of GPU and more powerful CPU make a deep neural network learning a reality!

Moore's Law claims that computing power doubles every two years. It has been true for a long time. Even though the trend is slowing down in recent years, it doesn't mean that the growth in computing power is over. The computing power will keep increasing at an impressive rate in the foreseeable future.

With those two major trends continues, we would like to claim that deep learning era is coming, and will stay.

Now, it is the right time to learn the new skill set and stay current!

Chapter 2

What is deep learning

Remember our previous definition for deep learning: it is a class of machine learning algorithms that uses multiple layers to progressively extract higher level features from the raw input.

The word "deep" in "deep learning" refers to the number of layers through which the data is transformed.

When we say deep learning, we usually refer to deep neural network (DNN) learning.

Let's start with the concept of the neural network, then we will talk about the learning process of DNN.

2.1 Neurual network

Here's a diagram for a typical feed-forward neural network :

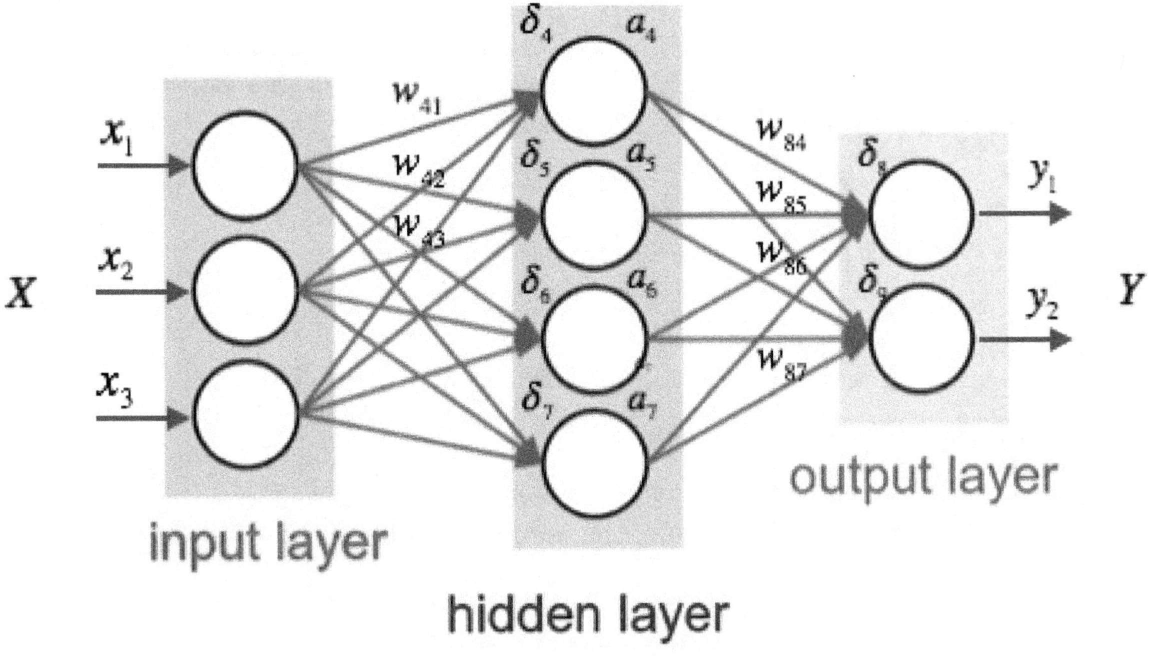

Figure 2.1: feedforward neural network diagram

It has:

- input layer, normally the raw input data, e.g.: images, video, voice data will be the input for this layer.
- several hidden layers, which are called neural network.
  If there are many hidden layers, we call it deep neural network (DNN).
- output layer, which output the final result.

For example: an image of cat or dog can be fed into the input layer, then processed by the hidden layer, finally, "cat or dog" will be classified by the output layer.

Tip

How many layers does a network need to have in order to qualify as deep? There is no official answer. Normally, a DNN has at least 2-3 hidden layers. It is not a surprise to see a 20 or 150-layer DNN in practice.

Inside the neural network, there are many nodes. Each node is called **neutron**, it has:

- its own input, which is a combination of the previous layer's outputs.
  For example: in the previous diagram, the input for a_4 is:
  $W_{41} * x_1 + W_{42} * x_2 + W_{43} * x_3$
  where W_{41}/W_{42} are called **weights**,
  which are the parameters that are learned/adjusted/trained by the sample data.
- an activation function, which generates output based on the input,
  e.g: f(z) = 1 / (1 + exp (-z))
  Normally, it's a non-linear function. The **non-linearity** enable a DNN to describe complicated behaviors. As you can imagine, if there are many layers in the neural network, there could be many parameters/weights.

Tip

What is neural network's capacity? The number of learnable parameters in a network/model is often referred to as the model's capacity/size. In the ideal world, we just want to specify the right size of a model (no less, but no more as well) in the network, but in reality, it hard to know. So the general workflow is to start with relatively a few layers and parameters, then increase the size of the layers or add new layers until you see diminishing returns with regard to validation loss.

2.2 Universal approximation theorem

Recall a function in mathematics:

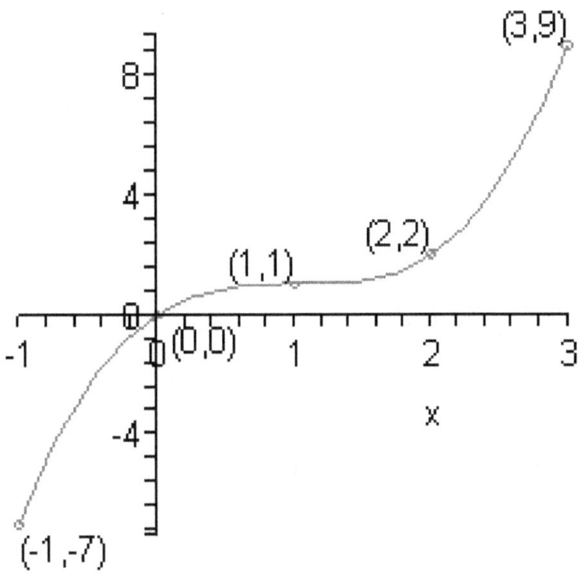

Figure 2.2: a mathematical function

y = f(x), where x is the input vector, the y is the output vector.

What a function defined is: for every input x, the function f generates or outputs y.

Almost everything in our world could be described by a function.

The neural network works like a function: the input/output layer is equivalent to x/y in a function, while the hidden layers is similar to the inside part of the function.

A pre-trained neural network is a such function, which outputs correct Y given certain X. The training process of a neural network is a systematic way to find such a function step by step!

Our brilliant mathematicians have proved a very striking fact: a neural network (even a single layer) can compute/simulate any function!

This is called **universal approximation theorem**.

Quote from Wikipedia:

```
In the mathematical theory of artificial neural networks,
the universal approximation theorem states that a feed-forward network
with a single hidden layer containing a finite number of neurons
can approximate continuous functions
on compact subsets of Rn, under mild assumptions on the activation function.
The theorem thus states that simple neural networks can represent
a wide variety of interesting functions when given appropriate parameters;
however, it does not touch upon the algorithmic learnability of those parameters.

George Cybenko proved one of the first versions of the theorem
in 1989 for sigmoid activation functions.

Kurt Hornik showed in 1991 that it is not the specific choice of the
activation function, but rather the multilayer feedforward architecture
itself which gives neural networks the potential of being
universal approximators.
```

This theorem not only indicated why neural network works in theory, but also shed some lights why we normally need to use multi-layer/deep neural networks in practice.

In fact, a training process of a neural network is an algorithmic way to learn those parameters!

Tip

Why different NN architectures?

We tend to use different NN architectures for different issues simply because we have specific intuitions/domain expertise for different issues. By putting the prior knowledge into the NN architecture, we hope it can simplify the issue, reduce computing complexity.

2.3 Deep learning process

How those parameters are learned?

At high level, the process of deep learning (supervised) is quite simple.

For example, we have one problem to solve, e.g: speech to text

- First, we need to collect many data point: input x, and labeled output y.
  In this case, x means a recorded audio, while y means the text associated with x. Usually, we split those data into a training set (60%), validation set (20%), testing set (20%).

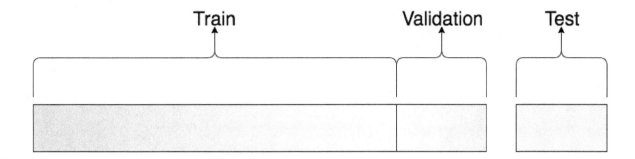

Figure 2.3: dataset split for training, validation, and tests

- Next, we design a neural network/model suited for this problem based on our previous experience. In this case, we chose LSTM (long short-term memory) network/model.
- Then, we feed the training data into the network, compare the output from the network and the expected output. Based on the difference, we can use some algorithms (e.g: backpropagation) to fine-tune those parameters.
- During the training, we use the validation data set to validate our model.
- If the error rate is high, we continue to fine-tune our model.
- If the error rate is acceptable, we skip the training loop, will use this trained model/parameters to predict testing data.
- Lastly, we use test data set to test our model.

The following is the pseudo-code of the deep learning process:

```
for each model    # may just have one model
    for each epoch
        for each training data instance
            propagate error(predicted - target) through the network
            based on the error, adjust the weights in the model
            calculate the accuracy over training data

        # now trained in this epoch, let's check how good it is
        for each validation data instance
            calculate the accuracy over the validation data
```

```
        if the threshold validation accuracy is met
            exit training
        else
            continue training

    # validation dataset said the model is good
    # let's check with testing data set
    test against test set, good? use it.
    if not, try to look how to adjust model etc.

Lastly, we pick a best model, or
sometimes we use all models (ensemble)
```

2.3.1 How weights are really learned?

The key part in the previous process is "adjust weights". How are they adjusted?

To understand it, we need to use some math.

Let's look at a simple example, assuming the model is a linear function:

```
# input is (x, y), output is z
z = w1 * x  + w2 * y

w1, w2 are the parameters for that linear function.
```

We have training data set:
$(x_1, y_1, z_{1'}), (x_2, y_2, z_{2'}), \ldots,$

our goal is to find good (w_1,w_2) that can predict/fit z well.

With this simple linear model, we can predict z given (x,y) as following:

```
z1 = w1 * x1 + w2 * y1 , (1) where the real data point is: z1'
z2 = w1 * x2 + w2 * y2 , (2) where the real data point is: z2'

note: z1,z2 are our calculated/estimated result based on w1,w2.
```

Please be noted that the real data is: z1', z2', which may not be the same as z1, z2.

The discrepancies between the estimated output (z1, z2) and training set (z1', z2') tell us how good our parameters are learned/chosen.

In ML, a **cost function** is used to describe those discrepancies, which measures how good our parameters are learned.

For simplicity, we use squared error function as our cost function here.

```
cost_function =  ( (z1' - z1)^2 + (z2' - z2)^2 ) /2
```

As you can see, this cost function can measure how big discrepancy between our estimated data and real training set.

If we substitute previous z1, z2 into the cost function, we get:

```
cost_function(w1,w2)  = ( ( z1' - ( w1 * x1 + w2 * y1) )^2 /2
                      + ( ( z2' - ( w1 * x2 + w2 * y2) )^2 /2
```

Remember $(x_1,y_1,z_{1'})$,$(x_2,y_2,z_{2'})$ are just data points, thus the cost function now totally depends on (w_1, w_2).

Now the problem is reduced to find a good (w_1,w_2), that will minimize the cost function over the data set.

Generally, the cost function can be written as: E(w(ij)), where w(ij) denotes the weight between neuron i and j, i,j=0…N

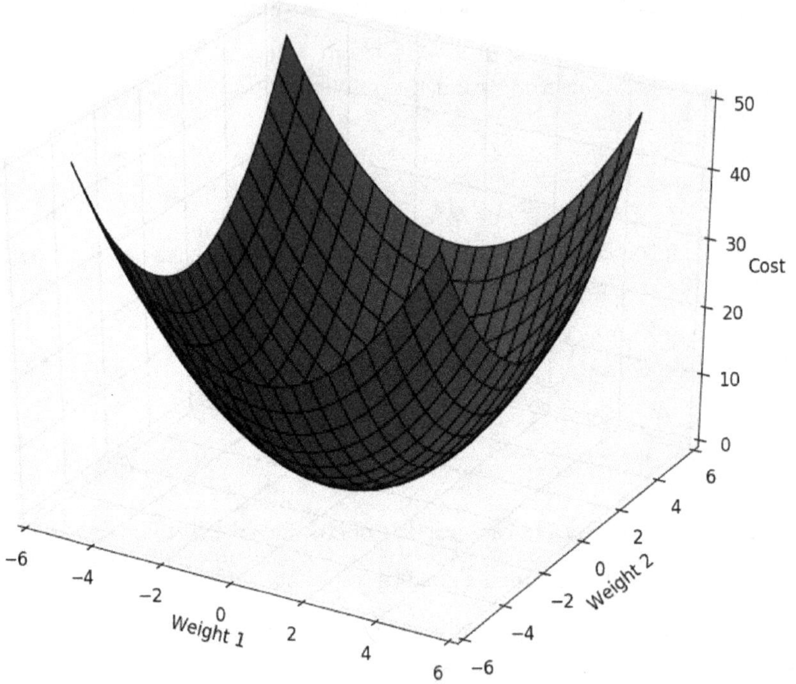

Figure 2.4: how to find minimum in weight space

If we plot cost function in the weight space, we can easily find the (w_1,w_2), that gives us the minimum cost. Our high-school/or college math tells us how to do it analytically by using **gradient descent**:

```
delta(cost_function E)/delta(w1) = 0;
```

```
delta(cost_function E)/delta(w2) = 0;
```

With those equations, we can get the optimum (w_1,w_2) analytically.

In many cases, the neural network/cost function are so complicated that we generally can not get those parameters analytically.

Fortunately, an awesome algorithm called **backpropagation** can help us find those parameters iteratively.

2.3.2 Backpropagation

The backpropagation algorithm can be dated back to the 1960s. In 1986, people realized that it can be applied in neural networks.

But only after the 2010s, people started to use backpropagation to solve real practical problems, thanks to the massive computing power provided by low-cost GPU-based systems.

Now backpropagation is one of the key algorithms in DNN.

In short, **backpropagation is a generalization of the delta rule to multi-layered feedforward networks by using the chain rule to iteratively compute gradients for each layer.**

Remember from previous sections, the learning process is reduced as the following problem:

To minimize the cost function E(w(ij)) in the weights w(ij) space.
Or put another way, to find a point in w(ij) space so that E(w(ij)) is minimized.

Gradient descent is well-known as a first-order iterative optimization algorithm to find the minimum of a function.

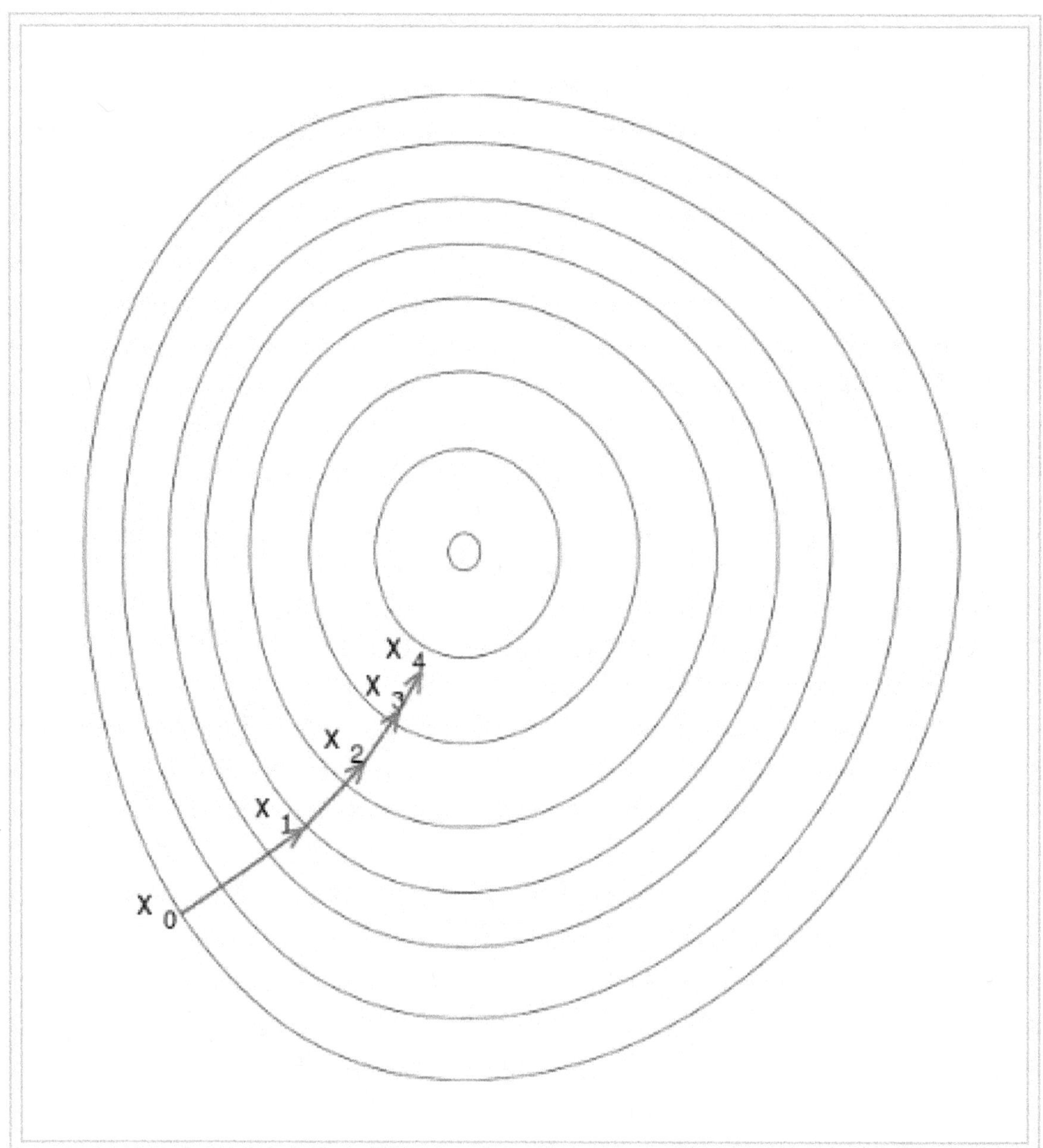

Figure 2.5: gradient descent to find minimum of a function

The figure showed how to find a minimum using gradient descent.

The way a computer finding a minimum is similar to the process showed in the previous figure. The key is to calculate gradients.

Backpropagation do help us to calculate those gradients.

It basically works like this:

- Assuming we use a logistic function as activation function and squared error as cost function E, we randomize w(i,j) initially,
- then we calculate the cost function's gradient with respect to w(i,j),
- with learning rate n >0, we will update w(i,j) for the next step by adding the following:

$$\Delta w_{ij} = -\eta \frac{\partial E}{\partial w_{ij}} = -\eta \delta_j o_i$$

where:

- $$\delta_j = \frac{\partial E}{\partial o_j} \frac{\partial o_j}{\partial \text{net}_j} = \begin{cases} (o_j - t_j) o_j (1 - o_j) & \text{if } j \text{ is an output neuron,} \\ (\sum_{\ell \in L} w_{j\ell} \delta_\ell) o_j (1 - o_j) & \text{if } j \text{ is an inner neuron.} \end{cases}$$
- $$o_j = \varphi(\text{net}_j) = \varphi\left(\sum_{k=1}^{n} w_{kj} o_k\right).$$
- t_j is target output for a training sample,
- L is a subset of neurons receiving input from neuron j.

If you read these equations carefully (especially those subscript, j, w_{jl}), you will find that we calculate the gradients from output layer back to the initial input layer. Thus, the name backpropagation!

As you see, we also need o_j as well, thus in the real backpropagation implementation, we generally calculate forward once to get those o_j, then calculate backward for those gradients.

Tip

Where/when to stop the update? Convergence to a local minimum can be guaranteed. When the function F is convex, all local minimum are also a global minimum, so in this case, gradient descent can converge to the global solution.

I intentionally neglected induction steps of how to get those equations in order to give you a high-level understanding of backpropagation.

You are encouraged to read it at:

https://en.wikipedia.org/wiki/Backpropagation

I found it is probably the cleanest/most concise descriptions of how backpropagation works.

A step by step example can be found at:

https://mattmazur.com/2015/03/17/a-step-by-step-backpropagation-example/

http://neuralnetworksanddeeplearning.com/chap2.html

2.4 Training, validation, test data set, error rate

To get a better insight into ML/DL, we need a deep understand of training, validation, testing data set.

2.4.1 Training Dataset

This data set is used to fit or train the model. In other words, during the training process, we adjust the parameters of a model according to this dataset.

For a neural network model, the parameters are normally the weights of connections between neurons in the network.

2.4.2 Validation Dataset

This data set is used to provide an unbiased evaluation of a model. Some people call it a **development set (dev set)**.

Usually, we use validation set to fine-tune model's hyperparameters, for example, the type of architecture of a model, the learning rate, or the number of training iterations, etc. They are totally different from model's internal parameters.

Validation datasets can be used for regularization such as early stopping as well. For example, we should stop training when the error rate on the validation dataset increases, as it is a sign of overfitting on the training dataset. This is essentially the same as fine-tuning the model's hyperparameters: the number of training iterations.

Tip
What is **over-fitting**?
It means that an empirical/apparent relationships identified in the training data set **do not hold in general**. Put another way, if over-fitting, the model only learned some specific things only applicable to the training data, but not general enough to apply to other data such as validation/test data. One obvious way to fight over-fitting is to enlarge training data set. Other techniques include: weight regularization, drop-out etc.

In short, we use the validation set to evaluate the performance of a model with different combinations of hyperparameters.

2.4.2.1 What is weight regularization?

Weight regularization works by adding a penalty associated with large weight to the loss function of the network, thus forcing NN's weights to take only small values. Doing so, we essentially place constraints on the quantity and type of information our model can store. If a network can only afford to memorize a small number of patterns, the optimization process will force it to focus on the most prominent patterns, which have a better chance of generalizing well.

Another angle to understand why this technique works could be explained by **Occam's Razor principle**, which is: Given two explanations for something, the simplest explanation that that makes the least amount of assumption is most likely to be correct one.

This principle could apply to the models learned by neural networks as well: given some training data and a network architecture, there are multiple sets of weights values (multiple models) that could explain the data, and simpler models are less likely to overfit than complex ones.

A "simple model" in this context is a model where the distribution of parameter values has less entropy (or a model with fewer parameters altogether).

The weight regularization put constraints on the complexity of a network by forcing its weights only to take small values, which makes the distribution of weight values more "regular", thus less entropy as distribution of those weight values are more restricted.

To give you concrete example. Assuming model 1 has parameters (1,1,1), while model 2 has parameters (1,2,3).

The model 1 is simpler because its distribution is the same, all parameters is 1, thus: p = 100% for value 1; while for model 2, we have three different values: p1 = 1/3 for 1, p2 = 1/3 for 2, p3 = 1/3 for 3.

Remember **entropy** is defined as: Sum($p_i \log(1/p_i)$), thus the entropy of model 1 is: 0, while the entropy of model 2 is: 3log(3). Obviously, model 1 has less entropy.

2.4.3 Cross-validation

Sometimes, we may hear people talk about cross-validation. What is it?

As we know, we normally split training data into training set and validate set according to some split ration (usually 70%/30% split). This is known as the **holdout method**. Some people view this as one of simplest kind of cross validation.

Well, as you can imagine, we could do a hold out process multiple times. For example, we can repeatedly partition the original training dataset into a training dataset and a validation dataset, but each time we the split differently. This is known as **cross-validation**, sometimes called **rotation estimation** or **out-of-sample testing**.

The cross-validation set can be used to help detect over-fitting and assist in hyper-parameter search.

Tip

What is **k-fold validation**?

It is a resampling procedure used to evaluate models on a limited data set. Usually the data is split into K partitions of equal size. For each partition i we train a model on the remaining K – 1 partitions, then evaluate it on partition i. The final score is the averages of the K scores obtained.

Tip

What is **iterated k-fold validation with shuffling**?

It consists of applying K-fold validation multiple times, shuffling the data every time before splitting. It is very helpful if we have a relatively small dataset.

The hold-out method is good to use when we have a very large dataset. In case of small dataset, cross-validation is usually the preferred method because it gives our model the opportunity to train on multiple train-test splits.

2.4.4 Test Dataset

This dataset is independent of the training dataset, but **follows the same probability distribution** as the training dataset.

The test data set is used to provide an unbiased evaluation of a final model fitting on the training dataset.

For example, if we have several models, how do we know the selected model is better than other different models? That's what the test data is for.

Roughly speaking, we can use the test data to evaluate the performance of the model, and use it to see if this model is useful or not.

Tip

Why we cannot compare model based on the validation set?

It because that validation set was part of the fitting process, remember, We used it to select the hyperparameter values!

2.5 Data pre-processing

A very important step in practice is data pre-processing.

The goal of data pre-processing is to make the raw data more amenable to neural networks.

It includes data vectorization, normalization, handling missing values, and feature extraction etc.

2.5.1 data vectorization

Neural network only knows the numeric number, so in this step we need to turn the high-level concepts into a numeric data.

For example, we need to denote class cat as numeric 1, dog as 2, etc.

Furthermore, those numeric data could be put into a more data-condensed/data-friendly format called **matrix**.

Many modern CPUs/GPUs are **vector processor**. They have "vector" instruction sets, which can apply the same operation simultaneously to two, four, or more pieces of data.

By converting data into matrix, we can not only write simpler code from software point of view, but also use many ML libraries e.g. NumPy that take advantages of CPU/GPU's vectorized arithmetic.

2.5.2 data normalization

It is generally not good to feed data with relatively large value into a neural network.

The best practice is to make sure each feature:

- independently to have a mean of 0.
- have a standard deviation of 1.

This is what data normalization tries to achieve.

2.5.3 handling missing data

We are not living in a perfect world. It is not uncommon that some data may be missing from the original dataset.

As a rule of thumb, if 0 is not a meaningful value in the dataset, we generally replace missing values with 0.

The powerful neural network will learn from the data set that the value 0 means missing data, and will start ignoring that value.

2.5.4 feature extraction

It is the process of transforming the input data into a set of features which can well represent the input data.

It is a special form of **dimensionality reduction**.

Many times, it is not that easy to find a good feature for our problems.

The good news is that generally, DNN is able to extract useful features automatically from raw data, thus remove the need of feature engineering in many cases.

But if we do know good features based on our domain knowledge, we should take advantage of them, as they allow us to solve problems less resources/data.

2.6 Summary

This chapter introduced many basic key concepts in deep learning.

In particular, you should know:

- what is a deep neural network.
- what is universal approximation theorem.
- how deep learning really learned,
- what is backpropagation, where/why is used in DNN.
- what are training, validation, test data set.
- what is data pre-processed, and how is normally pre-processed.

Chapter 3

Deep neural network components, layers

In this chapter, we will learn basic terms, concepts building blocks/components for a typical deep neural network.

3.1 activation functions

As we know, each neuron has an input, activation function, and output.

The activation function is key component in a neuron, it defines how to calculate the output from an input.

Normally, an activation function is a **non-linear function**, why?
The non-linearity allows the model to access a much richer hypothesis space or deep representation.

There are many activation functions. Which activation function should be chosen for our specific problem?

The standard answer is: it depends.

I listed frequently used activation functions here. The descriptions and comments inside each section could help you to build up some intuitions of how to choose an activation function.

You may read them briefly first, use them as references later.

3.1.1 sigmoid

Sigmoid function (also called **logistic function**) is one of the most used activation functions today.

It can be written as:

f(x) = 1/ (1 + exp(-x))

Sigmoid has a characteristic "S"-shaped curve or sigmoid curve, and a smooth gradient.

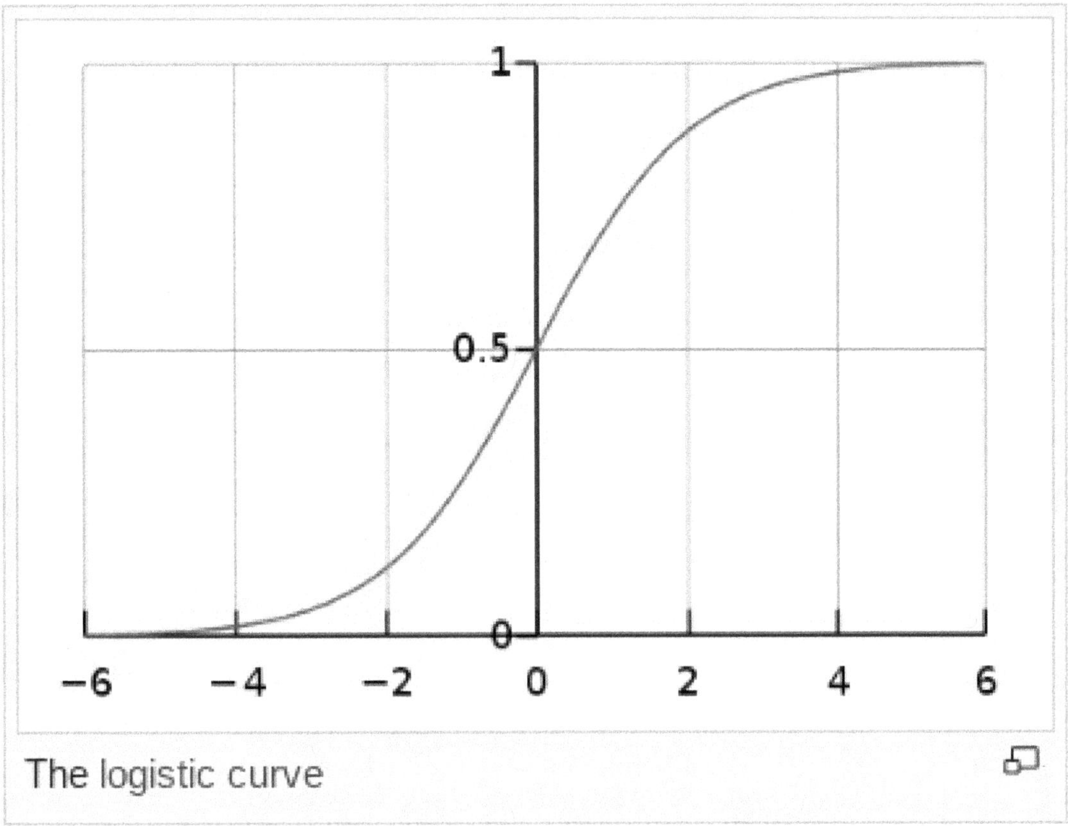

Figure 3.1: sigmoid function

One advantage of this nonlinear activation function is: its output will always be between (0,1).

That is great, as it won't blow up the activations.

Many natural processes, such as those complex system learning curves, exhibit a progression behavior: it starts from small beginnings, then speeds up, finally it approaches a climax.

Sigmoid can fit those processes well.

When a specific mathematical model is lacking, a sigmoid function is often used.

Well, are there any problems with this function?

You may notice that its gradient becomes smaller once x becomes larger. This gives rise to a problem called **vanishing gradients**. The backpropagation algorithm depends on gradients to give feedback to the system to adjust/update the parameters. If the gradient is tiny when input x is a large range, that means the neural network can NOT to learn further.

3.1.2 tanh

Tanh (also named hyperbolic tangent) is another very popular and widely used activation function.

It can be defined as:

$f(x) = \tanh x = (e^x - e^{(-x)}) / (e^x + e^{(-x)})$

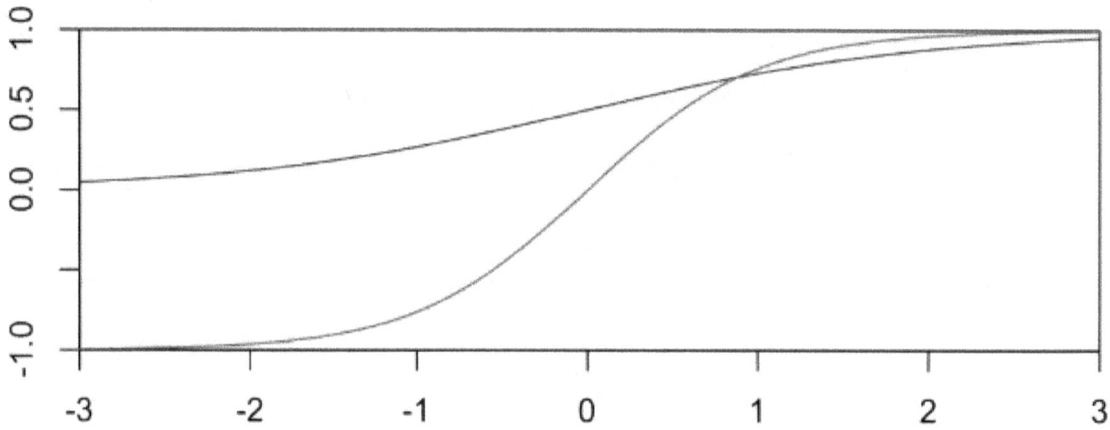

Figure 3.2: tanh function (blue is sigmoid, red is tanh)

Tanh looks very similar to sigmoid. In fact, it is a scaled sigmoid function!

Tanh has a stronger gradient (derivatives are steeper) than sigmoid. Deciding between the sigmoid or tanh depends on your requirement of gradient strength.

Like sigmoid, tanh has the vanishing gradient problem too.

3.1.3 softmax

Softmax is called normalized exponential function in mathematics.

In probability theory, the output of a softmax function can be used to represent a categorical distribution, a probability distribution over K different outcomes.

If we take an input of [1, 2, 3, 4, 1, 2, 3], the softmax can be calculated using the following formula:

$$\sigma(\mathbf{z})_j = \frac{e^{z_j}}{\sum_{k=1}^{K} e^{z_k}} \quad \text{for } j = 1, \ldots, K.$$

Figure 3.3: softmax function

The z_k refers to one of the inputs, e.g: 1. Thus, the softmax of that input will be:

[0.024, 0.064, 0.175, 0.475, 0.024, 0.064, 0.175].

The output has most of its weight where the *4* was in the original input. This is what the function is normally used for: **to highlight the largest values and suppress values which are significantly below the maximum value**.

Please note: softmax is not scale invariant, so if the input were [0.1, 0.2, 0.3, 0.4, 0.1, 0.2, 0.3] (which sums to 1.6) the softmax would be [0.125, 0.138, 0.153, 0.169, 0.125, 0.138, 0.153]. This shows that for values between 0 and 1, softmax in fact **de-emphasizes the maximum value** (note that 0.169 is not only less than 0.475, it is also less than the initial value of 0.4).

The softmax function is often used as the classifier in the final layer of a NN. Such networks are commonly trained under a log loss (or cross-entropy) regime, given a non-linear variant of multinomial logistic regression.

3.1.3.1 What is multinomial logistic regression?

First, do not confused Logistic regression with Linear regression.

Linear regression is used to predict the continuous dependent variable using a given set of independent variables.

While **Logistic regression** is a supervised learning classification algorithm used to predict the probability of a target variable (or dependent variable).

Tip
target variable or dependent variable?
One confusing part in ML/DNN is its practitioners often use multiple terms to refer to the same thing.
For example, in the ML/AI field, the variable being predicted is the output variable or the target variable. To a statistician, it is the **dependent variable** or the response.

Based on those number of categories of the target, Logistic regression can be divided into:

- Binary/Binomial: target have only two possible types either 1 and 0.
- Multinomial: target can have 3 or more possible unordered types or the types having no quantitative significance.

So Roughly speaking, multinomial logistic regression means a multi-class classification problem.

3.1.4 ReLu

ReLu (rectified linear unit), as of 2018, is the most popular activation function for deep neural networks, and it has been demonstrated that this function enables better training of deeper networks in 2011.

ReLu can be defined as:

f(x) = max(0,x)

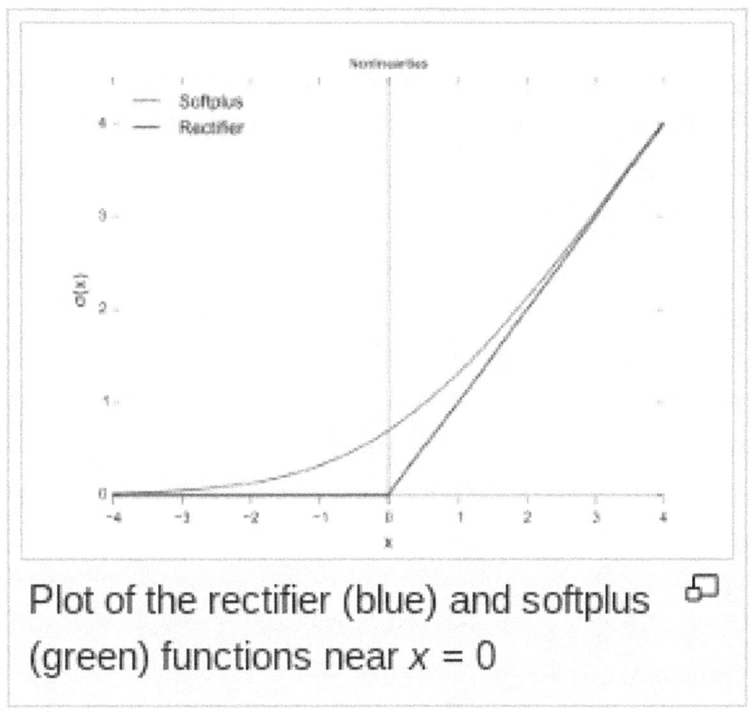

Softplus
Rectifier
Plot of the rectifier (blue) and softplus (green) functions near x = 0

Figure 3.4: relu and softplus function

It gives an output x if x is positive and 0 otherwise. The range of ReLu is [0, inf).

This means it can blow up the activation. It is nonlinear in nature.

Any function can be approximated with combinations of ReLu.

ReLu is less computationally expensive than tanh and sigmoid because it involves simpler mathematical operations.

ReLu gives us another good benefit called **sparsity of the activation**.
Imagine a ReLu network with randomly initialized weights, due to ReLu's property, almost half of the network yields 0 activations. That means fewer neurons are firing (sparse activation), thus the network is lighter.

However, ReLu has a problem called **dying ReLu problem**. As you can see, the gradient is 0 with negative X. That means some neurons will stop responding to variations in error/ input simply because the gradient is 0, nothing changes. This problem can cause several neurons to just die, and not respond, make a substantial part of the network passive.

There are variations in ReLu to mitigate this issue by simply making the horizontal line into a non-horizontal component. The main idea is to let the gradient be non-zero, and recover during training eventually.

3.1.4.1 softplus

softplus is a smooth approximation to the rectifier:

$f(x) = \log(1+e^x)$

3.1.4.2 Leaky ReLu

It is a variation of ReLu to mitigate the dying ReLu problem.

```
f(x)  = x if x > 0

        0.01x otherwise
```

3.1.4.3 Exponential linear unit (ELUs)

ELU is another variation of ReLu.

```
f( a, x)  = x   for x >0

            a *  ( exp(x)  - 1 ) otherwise
```

3.1.4.4 other variations of ReLus

There are many other variations of ReLus.

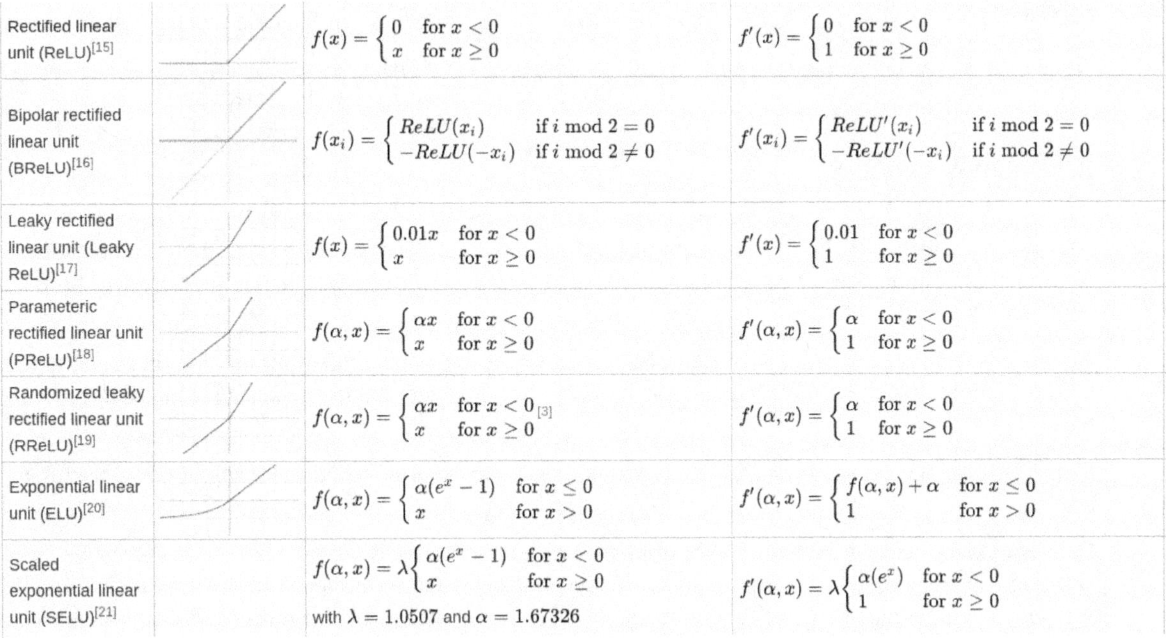

Rectified linear unit (ReLU)[15]		$f(x) = \begin{cases} 0 & \text{for } x < 0 \\ x & \text{for } x \geq 0 \end{cases}$	$f'(x) = \begin{cases} 0 & \text{for } x < 0 \\ 1 & \text{for } x \geq 0 \end{cases}$
Bipolar rectified linear unit (BReLU)[16]		$f(x_i) = \begin{cases} ReLU(x_i) & \text{if } i \bmod 2 = 0 \\ -ReLU(-x_i) & \text{if } i \bmod 2 \neq 0 \end{cases}$	$f'(x_i) = \begin{cases} ReLU'(x_i) & \text{if } i \bmod 2 = 0 \\ -ReLU'(-x_i) & \text{if } i \bmod 2 \neq 0 \end{cases}$
Leaky rectified linear unit (Leaky ReLU)[17]		$f(x) = \begin{cases} 0.01x & \text{for } x < 0 \\ x & \text{for } x \geq 0 \end{cases}$	$f'(x) = \begin{cases} 0.01 & \text{for } x < 0 \\ 1 & \text{for } x \geq 0 \end{cases}$
Parameteric rectified linear unit (PReLU)[18]		$f(\alpha, x) = \begin{cases} \alpha x & \text{for } x < 0 \\ x & \text{for } x \geq 0 \end{cases}$	$f'(\alpha, x) = \begin{cases} \alpha & \text{for } x < 0 \\ 1 & \text{for } x \geq 0 \end{cases}$
Randomized leaky rectified linear unit (RReLU)[19]		$f(\alpha, x) = \begin{cases} \alpha x & \text{for } x < 0 \\ x & \text{for } x \geq 0 \end{cases}$ [3]	$f'(\alpha, x) = \begin{cases} \alpha & \text{for } x < 0 \\ 1 & \text{for } x \geq 0 \end{cases}$
Exponential linear unit (ELU)[20]		$f(\alpha, x) = \begin{cases} \alpha(e^x - 1) & \text{for } x \leq 0 \\ x & \text{for } x > 0 \end{cases}$	$f'(\alpha, x) = \begin{cases} f(\alpha, x) + \alpha & \text{for } x \leq 0 \\ 1 & \text{for } x > 0 \end{cases}$
Scaled exponential linear unit (SELU)[21]		$f(\alpha, x) = \lambda \begin{cases} \alpha(e^x - 1) & \text{for } x < 0 \\ x & \text{for } x \geq 0 \end{cases}$ with $\lambda = 1.0507$ and $\alpha = 1.67326$	$f'(\alpha, x) = \lambda \begin{cases} \alpha(e^x) & \text{for } x < 0 \\ 1 & \text{for } x \geq 0 \end{cases}$

Figure 3.5: variations of ReLus functions

3.1.5 other activation functions

A complete list can be found at:

https://en.wikipedia.org/wiki/Activation_function

3.1.6 How to choose an activation function?

As a general rule: we should choose an activation function approximate the characteristics of the problem we are trying to solve.

For example, a sigmoid may work better for a classifier because approximating a classifier function as combinations of sigmoid is easier than ReLu. Thus lead to faster training process and convergence.

Softmax is typically used only in the output layer of a neural network to represent a probability distribution of possible outcomes of the network.

Otherwise, we can start with ReLu and its variations, which works most of the time as a general approximator.

Of course, we can define our own custom activation function if it makes sense.

3.2 DNN Layers

As we learned before, a DNN have many hidden layers. Each layer could be different, and performs different functionality. Those layers are the building blocks of a DNN. A different DNN architecture will have a different combination of different layers.

Not surprisingly, designing a DNN is similar to building a toy using LEGO blocks. We first need to know what kind of building blocks are available in our toolbox. So let's learn some typical DNN building blocks, in DNN terms, layers.

Convolutional neural network (CNN) is a great starting point as it introduced many different useful layers/concepts.

CNNs or ConvNets have been the source of many major breakthroughs in deep learning in the last few years. They are used primarily to look for patterns in an image. For example, for a typical image classification problem, the first few layers will identify lines and corners, the later layers will recognize more complex/abstract features, the last layer normally output the desired classification.

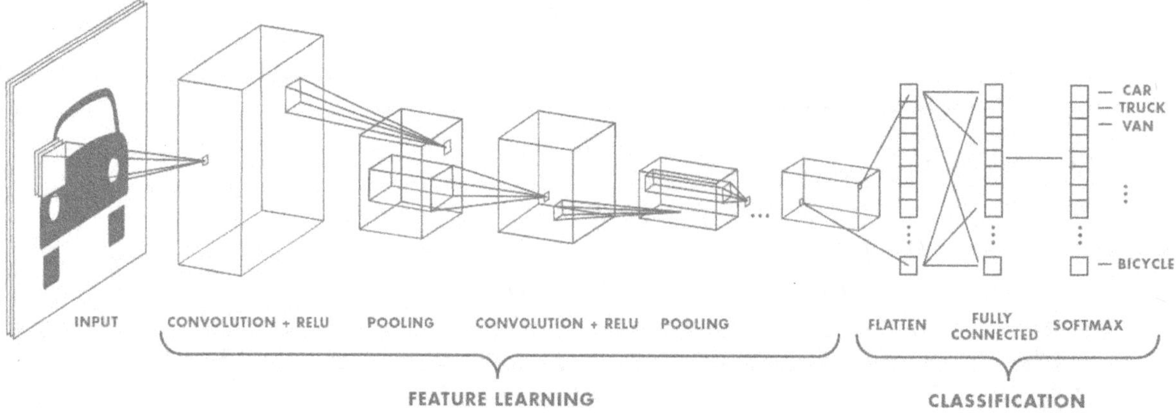

Figure 3.6: a typical CNN architecture

As shown in the figure above, a typical CNN contains convolutional, pooling, activation, fully-connected layers etc.

3.2.1 convolutional layer

Convolutional layer (conv layer) is one of the most important layers in CNN. It is convoluting over an image and looking for patterns.

For example, we have a 28x28 image represented by a 28x28 matrix, then, we take a 3x3 matrix, slide that 3x3 window around the image. At each position the 3x3 window visits, we matrix multiply the values of 3x3 window by the values in the image that are currently being covered by the window. This is called **convolution operation**.

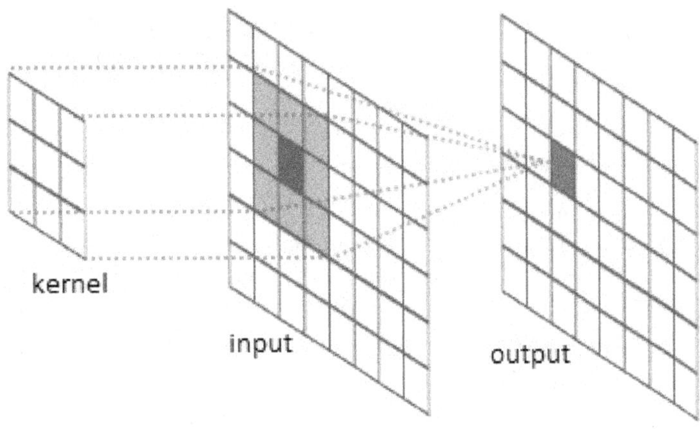

Figure 3.7: convolution operation

The window (3x3 matrix) that moves over the image is called a **kernel** which is typically a square matrix. The distance the window moves each time is called the **stride**. Additionally, images are sometimes padded with zeros (could avg or max) around the perimeter when performing convolutions, that is called **padding**.

As the window sliding over the image, we will compute the convolution for each move, thus generates a smaller matrix called convolved **feature matrix**. Each data point in the feature matrix corresponds to a section of the image.

From a pure mathematics point of view, convolution is a mathematical operation on two functions (f and g) to produce a third function that expresses how the shape of one is modified by the other.

$$(f * g)(t) \triangleq \int_{-\infty}^{\infty} f(\tau)g(t-\tau)\,d\tau$$

Figure 3.8: convolution definition

A convolutional layer could be seen as a **filter**. As we move over an image using a specific kernel, we check for patterns in that section of the image. Remember that kernel is defined by the weights in that matrix. When we train using an image, we will update/adjust these weights so that our cost function is minimized. When we evaluate an image by using convolution operation with that filter, the network (of that layer) will output high values if it matches a pattern trained before.

As you can imagine, it is possible that the combinations of various filters/layers will allow the network to predict the content of an image. The learning process in this case is to adjust/update those filters.

Here is how CNN works from high-level point of view: the first convolution layer will learn small local patterns such as edges, the second convolution layer will use those edges to detect textures, the third layer will use the textures to detect patterns, the fourth layer will use the patterns to detect parts of objects, The next layer will learn larger patterns made of the features of the previous layers, and so on. Thus, convnets can efficiently learn increasingly complex, abstract visual concepts and spatial hierarchies of patterns.

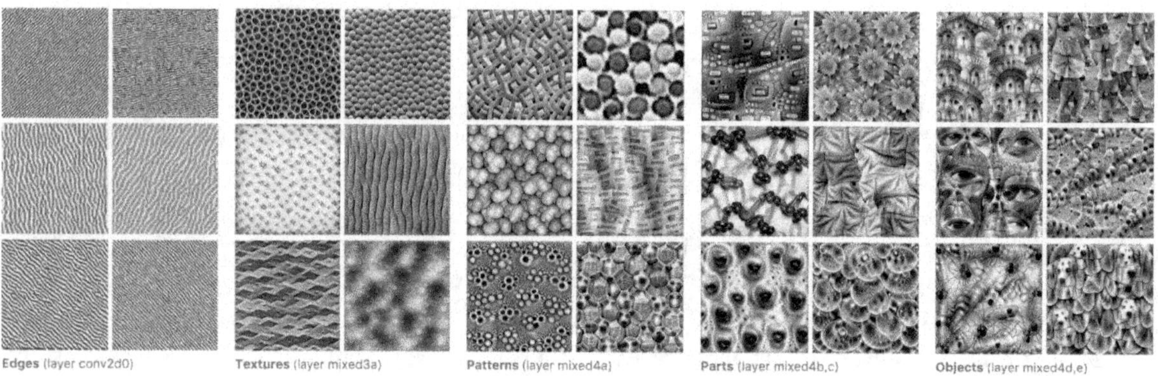

Figure 3.9: cnn filter visualization

The figure above showed the visualization of those layers.

More details can be found at:

https://distill.pub/2017/feature-visualization/

BTW, the patterns that convolution filters learned are translation/space invariant as the visual world is fundamentally translation/space invariant.

3.2.2 activation layer

In DNN, it is a convention to apply a **nonlinear layer** (or activation layer) immediately after each conv layer.

What it means is: we just pass the value (from the conv layer) to a function defined by the activation layer, which squashes that value into a certain range.

The purpose of this layer is to introduce non-linearity to a DNN system. Remember the conv layer is basically computed with linear operations (e.g. element-wise multiplications and summations).

The most popular activation function in CNNs is ReLu due to its low cost to compute, thus we can train the network faster.

3.2.3 pooling layer

Pooling layers could reduce the number of parameters if the images are too large.

Spatial pooling, called **subsampling** or **downsampling** reduces the dimensionality of each map, but retains the important information.

Max pooling and Average pooling are the most common pooling functions. **Max pooling** takes the largest value from the window of the image, while **average pooling** takes the average of all values in the window. **Sum Pooling** sums of all elements in the window.

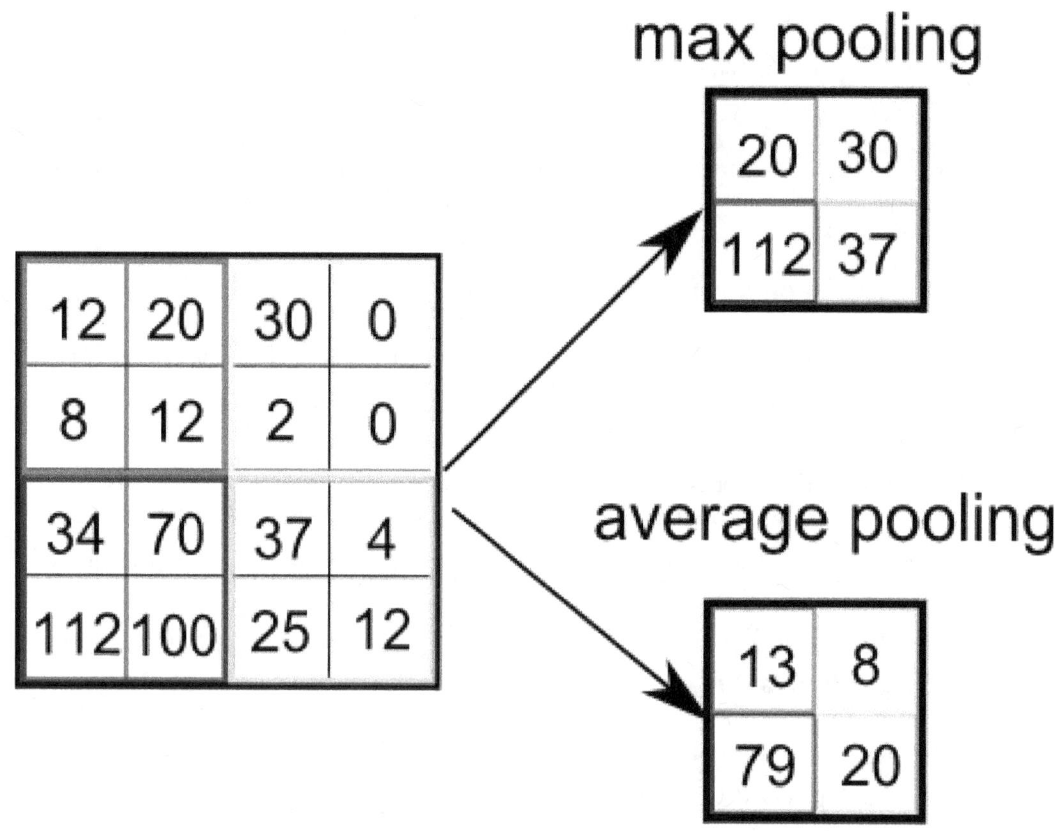

Figure 3.10: Max Pooling and Average Pooling

Max pooling tends to work better than others in many cases probably because the maximal value may reveal/emphasize more unique information in the feature space than the average does.

3.2.4 dropout layer

Dropout refers to ignoring some random units (i.e. neurons), during the training phase. More precisely, these units are not considered, thus ignored during a particular forward or backward pass compute.

It is one of the most effective and commonly used regularization technique to fight over-fitting.

It helps to reduce interdependent learning amongst the neurons.

You can read more at:

http://www.cs.toronto.edu/~rsalakhu/papers/srivastava14a.pdf

3.2.5 fully connected layers

A fully connected layer, also called densely connected layer or dense layer, connects every neuron in one layer to every neuron in another layer.

It is the same as the traditional **((multi-layer perceptron neural network))** (**MLP**) in principle.

One fundamental difference between a densely connected layer and a convolution layer is: **dense layers tend to learn global patterns in their input feature space, whereas convolution layers tent to learn local patterns.**

3.2.6 softmax layer

It is similar to the activation layer, we just apply softmax function on inputs. In CNN or many DNNs, it is often used in the final layer as a classifier.

3.2.7 other layers

There are many other layers such as: **flatten layer**, **embedding layer**, **merge layer**, **noise layer** etc, you probably can guess what those layers do.

We will discuss those layers in more detail later in our code examples.

3.3 summary

After reading this chapter, you should:

- have a basic understanding of many activation functions, specially ReLu, softmax, sigmoid, etc.
- know how to choose different activation functions.
- have a high-level understanding of different DNN layers, especially convolutional, softmax, dropout, pooling, and activation layer.

Chapter 4

Deep learning development environments

Powered by the basic knowledge from previous chapters, we actually can solve some real deep learning problems!

Well, starting everything from scratch is hard. Fortunately, there are many convenient open source/free deep learning frameworks/toolkits to make our life much easier.

To just name a few, Pytorch, Torch, Tensorflow/Keras, Theano, Caffe, MXNET, Microsoft Cognitive Toolkit etc are popular machine learning development frameworks.

Among them, Pytorch is emerging as a winner, especially among researchers due to python-first (deep integration into python), easy-to-debug, its capability of generating dynamic computation graphs, and a flexible low-level API to meet customization requirements etc. It is an open-source python machine learning library based on Torch, mainly developed by Facebook's artificial intelligence research group, and Uber's Pyro software.

Keras/Tensorflow is quite popular due to its ease of use, syntactic simplicity, facilitates fast development, especially for beginners. If Cuda/TensorFlow is like an assembly language, Keras is like Bash/shell, then Pytorch is right in the middle like C/C++, gives us a powerful, flexible, customizable, and debuggable framework without losing much on the ease of use.

In this book, we will use PyTorch as our development environment. It will help us build a deep insight into the DNN because it requires a significant understanding of neural network to write a working code!

Once we grasp the core concepts of deep learning in PyTorch, we can easily apply them elsewhere such as Keras/TensorFlow etc.

Now let's get set up a PyTorch environment.

4.1 Install PyTorch on your local box

Pytorch has an excellent document, you can easily follow the online installation guide to set it up.

The following is the screenshot of its online installation instruction:

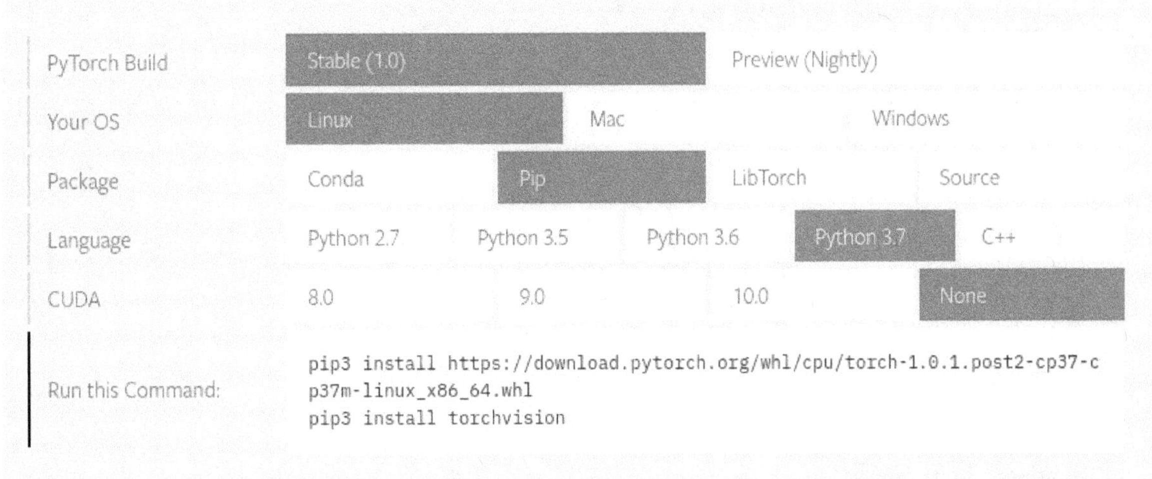

Figure 4.1: how to install pytorch

Please read it at:

https://pytorch.org/

or:

https://pytorch.org/get-started/locally/

Here are my steps on debian 9/10 just for your reference.

I will use a python3 virtual environment without a GPU.

4.1.1 install pytorch on python3 virtual environment

(1) install python3 virtual environment.

```
$ sudo apt-get install python3-venv

# create a python3 virtual environment
$ python3 -m venv pytorch-cpu

# Activate the Virtualenv environment:
$ source pytorch-cpu/bin/activate
```

(2) install pytorch according to the table at:

https://pytorch.org/get-started/locally/

```
(pytorch-cpu) $  pip3 install https://download.pytorch.org/whl/cpu/torch-1.0.1. ↩
    post2-cp37-cp37m-linux_x86_64.whl
(pytorch-cpu) $  pip3 install torchvision
```

(3) test the install

```
(pytorch-cpu) ~$ python
Python 3.7.2+ (default, Feb  2 2019, 14:31:48)
[GCC 8.2.0] on linux
Type "help", "copyright", "credits" or "license" for more information.
>>> import torch
>>> print(torch.__version__)
1.0.1.post2
>>> torch.cuda.is_available()
False
```

If you see no error, then you have installed pytorch successfully!

4.2 Use google's Colab

Google provides a very cool online tool called Colab to allow us to learn and experiment pytorch/keras/tensorflow for free!

The beauty of colab is: we do NOT need to install anything! It even provides free access to GPU and TPU (google's tensorflow processor) up to 12 hours (at the time of writing).

You'd better have a google account (it is free to sign up), as you may need to save the code/data/result into google drive.

In short, google's Colab provides a python Jupyter notebook-like environment, which works like a virtual machine.

You can access it at:
https://colab.research.google.com

PyTorch is already pre-installed and optimized for their hardware. Just import torch, you can start coding.

4.2.1 how to access colab's GPU

To access GPU, we need to change the notebook's runtime by clicking Runtime→change runtime type

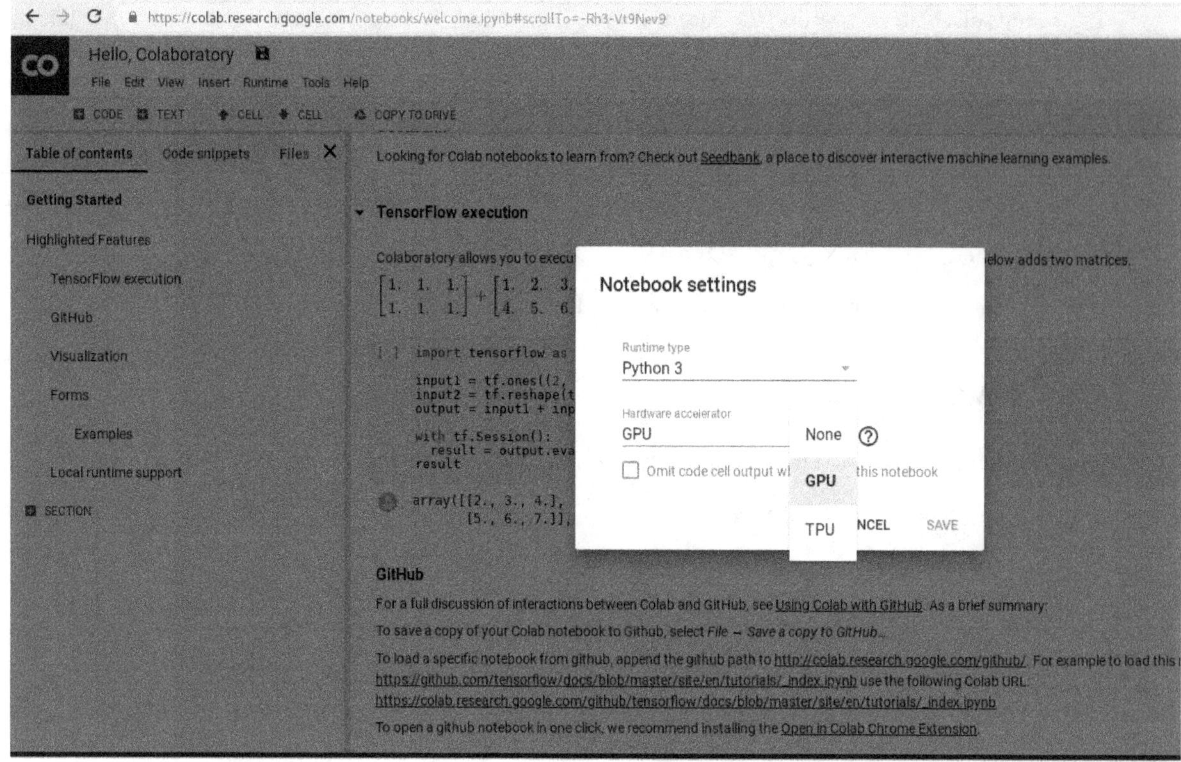

Figure 4.2: google colab runtime (free access to GPU)

Warning

If you choose TPU, pytorch cannot use it as GPU: torch.cuda.is_available() will return false. So you need to choose GPU instead of TPU for pytorch.

To run a pytorch example, you can just copy/paste pytorch code into the code cell, then hit the play button on the upper left corner of the code cell.

4.2.2 how to install additional lib

By default, Colab pre-installed many libraries already, but in case you need some additional libraries, you can install them using !pip install or !apt-get

For example,

```
# install python's pydot
!pip install pydot

# or install some os level package
!apt-get some_debian_pkg
```

4.2.3 colab with github access

Google Colab also supports github.

4.2.3.1 access python notebook in github

If you have a notebook in github, we can:

- To save a copy of your Colab notebook to Github, select File → Save a copy to GitHub...
- To load a specific notebook from github, append the github path to

http://colab.research.google.com/github/

For example, to load this notebook in Colab:

https://github.com/tensorflow/docs/blob/master/site/en/tutorials/_index.ipynb

You can use the following Colab URL:

https://colab.research.google.com/github/tensorflow/docs/blob/master/site/en/tutorials/_index.ipynb

More information can be found at:

https://colab.research.google.com/github/googlecolab/colabtools/blob/master/notebooks/colab-github-demo.ipynb

4.2.3.2 directly run project from github

Sometimes, we have python code in a github repo, we can clone and run it directly.

```
!git clone https://github.com/keras-team/keras
!ls
!python examples/addition_rnn.py
```

4.2.4 How to upload to colab and download file from colab

- Upload files from your local file system

```
from google.colab import files

# will prompt a file dialog
uploaded = files.upload()

for fn in uploaded.keys():
  print('User uploaded file "{name}" with length {length} bytes'.format(
      name=fn, length=len(uploaded[fn])))
```

- Download files to your local file system

```
from google.colab import files

with open('example.txt', 'w') as f:
  f.write('some content')

files.download('example.txt')
```

4.2.5 How to access google drive from colab

Here is a quick note on how to access google drive from google colab.

- Mounting Google Drive as the local drive in colab's virtual environment

```
from google.colab import drive
drive.mount('/content/gdrive')

with open('/content/gdrive/My Drive/foo.txt', 'w') as f:
  f.write('Hello Google Drive!')
!cat /content/gdrive/My\ Drive/foo.txt
```

You can find more information at:

https://colab.research.google.com/notebooks/io.ipynb

4.3 Jupyter notebook

The Jupyter Notebook is an open-source web application that allows you to create and share documents that contain live code, equations, visualizations, and narrative text.

It is especially useful to show the code and run results etc in deep learning. You probably will see many examples packaged as jupyter notebook instead of pure python code on the Internet.

Let's install it first.

```
# under your python virtual environment
(pytorch-cpu) pip install jupyter

# start a jupyter notebook
jupyter notebook
[I 12:49:11.448 NotebookApp] Serving notebooks from local directory: / ↩
    learning_pytorch/sources
[I 12:49:11.449 NotebookApp] The Jupyter Notebook is running at:
[I 12:49:11.449 NotebookApp] http://localhost:8888/?token=4 ↩
    d8e709f5d2bd546ff19a618c54cae6807686f3b9180e0dd
```

```
[I 12:49:11.449 NotebookApp] Use Control-C to stop this server and shut down all kernels (twice to skip confirmation).
[C 12:49:12.157 NotebookApp]

    To access the notebook, open this file in a browser:
        file:///run/user/1000/jupyter/nbserver-29457-open.html
    Or copy and paste one of these URLs:
        http://localhost:8888/?token=4d8e709f5d2bd546ff19a618c54cae6807686f3b9180e0dd
```

To use it, just use a browser to access the above URL. You should see similar content like:

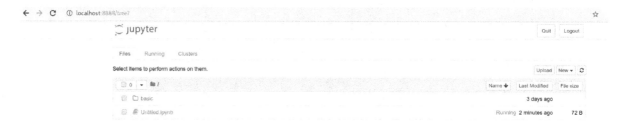

Figure 4.3: access jupyter notebook from a browser

Now on the top right button, you can click new→Python3 to open a new notebook, type some python code inside a cell, then type shift-enter to run it (or click cell→Run cells)

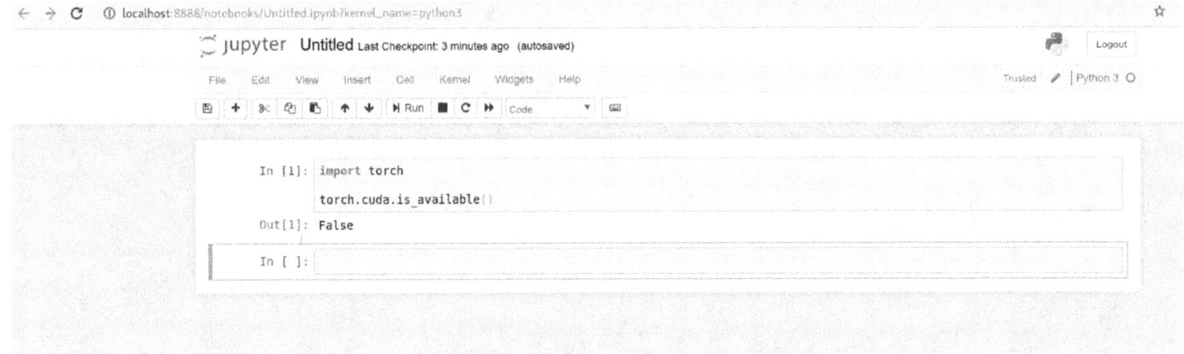

Figure 4.4: run a jupyter notebook

You can save it as a notebook (.ipynb), or open an existing notebook by clicking the File etc.

The interface is intuitive, easy to use.

More documents can be found at:

https://jupyter.org/documentation

Chapter 5

Python and Tensor basic

Python is probably the most popular language for machine learning. It's the main language that will be used in this book.

We assume you have basic knowledge about python. However, if you know little about it, but have some programming experience in any other computer languages, you should be able to pick it up quickly.

More information about the python can be found at:

https://www.python.org

Besides python, we need to have a fair amount of knowledge about **tensor**, which is a very important fundamental concept in ML.

If you know Python and tensor well, please skip this chapter.

In this chapter, we first highlight some basic, but useful python concepts related to ML, then we will introduce the key tensor concept.

Important

Please get familiar with those concepts!

5.1 Python basic

Python expression is normally natural intuitive, powerful, and overloaded.

But sometimes it can become quite confusing, and hard to know the exact meaning until you dig into the python reference documents.

Some confusing, but useful python terms are presented here, I hope it will help you to understand python code more precisely.

5.1.1 list, array, tuple

A **list** is a collection which is **ordered and changeable.**
It allows duplicate members.
In Python, lists are written with square brackets (e.g.: [ ]) .

The **array** is similar to list, but it is a python library. Both are good for the one-dimensional array. We will see the difference shortly after the example code.

A **tuple** is a collection which is **ordered and unchangeable.**
It allows duplicate members.
In Python, tuples are written with round brackets (e.g: ( )).

Now let's look at some examples:

```
# list, ordered and changeable, Allows duplicate members.
>>> d = [1,2,3,4,4,5, "word"]
>>> d
[1, 2, 3, 4, 4, 5, "word"]

# array, similar to list, all elements should have the same type
>>> import array
# the first parameter is typecode of this array,
# it means all the items in this array will have the same type,
# specified by this typecode, here 'l' means int in python
# https://docs.python.org/2/library/array.html
>>> c = array.array('l', [1, 2, 3, 4, 4,5])
>>> c
array('l', [1, 2, 3, 4, 4, 5])
```

```
# tuple, ordered but unchangeable, Allows duplicate members.
>>> t = (110, 10, 3, 3, "word")
>>> t
(110, 10, 3, 3)
```

What is the difference between list and array?

Python lists are very flexible and can hold completely heterogeneous arbitrary data. They can be appended to very efficiently, in amortized constant time. If you need to shrink and grow your array time-efficiently without hassle, the lists are the way to go. But they use a lot more space than C arrays.

The array.array type from the array library, on the other hand, is just a thin wrapper on C arrays. It can hold only homogeneous data, all items need to be the same type, and it only uses sizeof(one object) * length bytes of memory.

Thus a list can be something like:

```
[1, 'a', [1, 2], 'string']
```

While an array can only contain things of the same type:

```
[1, 2, 3, 4]
```

5.1.2 set, dict

A **set** is a collection which is **unordered and unindexed.**
No duplicate members are allowed.
In Python, sets are written with curly brackets (e.g. { }).

A dictionary is a collection that is **unordered, changeable and indexed.**
No duplicate members are allowed.
In Python, dictionaries are written with the same curly brackets as set , but the format is different, it has keys and values (e.g. { "first name": "my name"}).

Please see the following example for the difference.

```
# set, unordered and unindexed. No duplicate members.
>>> s = { 1, 2, 3, "word" }
>>> s
{1, 2, 3, "word"}

# to get the intersection between a set and a list.
>>> new_set = myset.intersection(mylist)

# dictionary, unordered, changeable, and indexed, No duplicate members.
>>> dict = { "first name": "first", 1:"last", "year": 1988}
>>> dict
{'year': 1988, 1: 'last', 'first name': 'first'}
```

Warning

In python, we can mix number, string as element inside list/tuple/set/dictionary!

5.1.3 comprehension for list, set, dict

One nice feature in python is called **comprehension**, which enables people to write concise high-level, yet still understandable code.

It is quite useful, thus quite often appeared in many ML code/examples.

Comprehensions are constructs that allow sequences to be built from other sequences. Python 2.0 introduced list comprehensions, and Python 3.0 comes with dictionary and set comprehension.

Quote from the official python document: **List comprehensions** provide a concise way to create lists. Common applications are to make new lists where each element is the result of some operations applied to each member of another sequence or iterable, or to create a subsequence of those elements that satisfy a certain condition.

It is easier to learn the comprehension by examples.

```
# set comprehension example
# generate a list using comprehension
>>> a_list = [2*x for x in range(10) if x**2 > 3]
>>> a_list
```

```
[4, 6, 8, 10, 12, 14, 16, 18]

# let's append a string
>>> a_list.append("test")
>>> a_list
[4, 6, 8, 10, 12, 14, 16, 18, 'test']

# now use list comprehension to generate another list
>>> squared = [ x**2 for x in a_list if type(x) == int ]
>>> squared
[16, 36, 64, 100, 144, 196, 256, 324]

# If we observe the examples carefully,
# we probably can summarize the format of comprehension as:

[ output_function(x) for x in a_list if predicate_condition(x) ]
```

Similar to list comprehension, the following are some examples of set comprehension and dictionary comprehension.

```
# set comprehensions
>>> a_set = {1,2,3,"word"}
>>> a_set
{1, 2, 3, 'word'}
>>> sub_set = {x for x in a_set if type(x) == int}
>>> sub_set
{1, 2, 3}

#dictionary comprehensions
>>> a_dict = { "first name": "first", 1:"last", "year": 1988}
>>> a_dict
{'year': 1988, 1: 'last', 'first name': 'first'}

>>> sub_dict = { k:v for k,v in a_dict.items() if type(v) == int }
>>> sub_dict
{'year': 1988}
```

5.1.4 zip

In python comprehension, we may often see zip() especially when we deal with two or more elements at a time.

The **zip()** function returns an iterator of tuples.

Python iterator objects conform to the **iterator protocol**, which means they need to provide two methods: *iter*() and next().

The ***iter*** returns the iterator object, and is implicitly called at the start of loops.

The **next()** method returns the next value and is implicitly called at each loop increment. It raises a StopIteration exception when there is no more value to return, which in turn will be captured implicitly by looping constructs to stop iterating.

```
>>> x = [1, 2, 3]
>>> y = [4, 5, 6]

# access one iterator, v is an element from y
>>> [ 2*v for k,v in zip(x,y) ]
[8, 10, 12]

# here v itself is a tuple, in this example is: (1,4)
# when used *, it is gets repeated as (1,4,1,4)
# instead of multiplied by value.
>>> [ 2*v for v in zip(x,y) ]
[(1, 4, 1, 4), (2, 5, 2, 5), (3, 6, 3, 6)]

>>> zipped = zip(x, y)

# Converting iterator to list by calling a list constructor: list([iterable])
>>> list(zipped)
[(1, 4), (2, 5), (3, 6)]

# note, it is empty as zipped was an iterator, already at
# end of iterating
>>> list(zipped)
[]

# zip() in conjunction with the * operator can be used to unzip a list:
>>> x2, y2 = zip(*zip(x, y))
>>> x == list(x2) and y == list(y2)
True
```

5.1.5 how to inspect new class/obj

Sometimes, we know little about a new python obj/class, even online documents may not have many details. Fortunately, there are several built-in functions could help us with that.

- help([object]), it will give some good inside documents
- dir([object]), it is very useful to see what is inside the object.
- type()
- id()
- getattr()
- hasattr()
- globals()
- locals()
- callable()

For example, from Keras online documents, we do not know much about keras text preprocessing Tokenizer, let's use those built-in function to get more info:

```
>>> from keras.preprocessing.text import Tokenizer
>>> t = Tokenizer()

# most useful
>>> dir(t)
['__class__', '__delattr__', '__dict__', '__dir__', '__doc__', '__eq__', '__format__', '__ge__', '__getattribute__', '__gt__', '__hash__', '__init__', '__le__', '__lt__', '__module__', '__ne__', '__new__', '__reduce__', '__reduce_ex__', '__repr__', '__setattr__', '__sizeof__', '__str__', '__subclasshook__', '__weakref__', 'char_level', 'document_count', 'filters', 'fit_on_sequences', 'fit_on_texts', 'index_docs', 'lower', 'num_words', 'oov_token', 'sequences_to_matrix', 'split', 'texts_to_matrix', 'texts_to_sequences', 'texts_to_sequences_generator', 'word_counts', 'word_docs', 'word_index']
>>> help(t)
```

```
Help on Tokenizer in module keras.preprocessing.text object:

class Tokenizer(builtins.object)
 |  Text tokenization utility class.
 |
 |  This class allows to vectorize a text corpus, by turning each
 |  text into either a sequence of integers (each integer being the index
 |  of a token in a dictionary) or into a vector where the coefficient
 |  for each token could be binary, based on word count, based on tf-idf...
...
>>> hasattr(t, "document_cou")
False
>>> hasattr(t, "document_count")
True
>>> getattr(t, "document_count")
10
```

5.1.6 generator function, generator expression

Another very useful and powerful function in python is called **generator function** or briefly **generator**. It allows us to declare a function that behaves like an iterator, which can be used in a python for loop.

Why do we need this?
In ML, we deal with lots of data, sometimes infinite data sequence, thus we can not load all data into memory. Python generator provides us a good way to write a memory-efficient, simplified, and understandable code for this problem. We will illustrate it in some example code later.

Actually, it is fairly simple to create a generator in Python. Instead of using return statement while defining a normal function, we replace it with a yield statement when we want to define a generator function.

The magic **yield** statement suspends function's execution, sends whatever specified by the yield back to the caller, at the same time, it retains enough state to enable the function to resume where it is left off. When resumed, the function continues execution immediately after the last yield run.

When a generator function is called, it returns an object (iterator) but does not start execution immediately.

Methods like *iter*() and *next*() are implemented automatically, so we can iterate through the items using next().

Let's look at an example:

```
# a generator that yields items instead of returning a list
>>> def firstn(n):
      num = 0
      while num < n:
        yield num
        num += 1 # Next execution resumes from here

>>> sum_of_first_n = sum(firstn(10))
>>> sum_of_first_n
45

>>> t = firstn(10)

# note t is generator obj!
>>> t
<generator object firstn at 0x7fd5cd68cd58>

# we can iterate through it by next()
>>> next(t)
0
>>> next(t)
1
>>> next(t)
2
# sum it
>>> sum(t)
42
# Why the sum is not 45?
# It is because it has already been iterated 3 times before we sum it.
# add all together we get the same result: 42 + 0 + 1 + 2 = 45

# now t can not generate any more data, it will be stopped!
>>> next(t)
Traceback (most recent call last):
  File "<stdin>", line 1, in <module>
StopIteration
```

Tip

a generator will provide performance benefits, only if we do not intend to use that set of generated values more than once, as it is intended to be used only once just like other iterators!

A **generator expression** provides a shortcut to build generators out of expressions. We can easily turn a list comprehension into a generator expression by replacing the square brackets ("[ ]") with parentheses. Alternately, we can think of list comprehensions as generator expressions wrapped in a list constructor.

It is better illustrated using the following example:

```
# a list comprehension
>>> l = [ x for x in range(10) ]
>>> l
[0, 1, 2, 3, 4, 5, 6, 7, 8, 9]
>>> sum(l)
45
>>> l
[0, 1, 2, 3, 4, 5, 6, 7, 8, 9]

# a generator expression ( using () instead of [] )
>>> tl = ( x for x in range(10) )
>>> tl
<generator object <genexpr> at 0x7fd5cd68cd58>
>>> next(tl)
0
>>> next(tl)
1
>>> next(tl)
2
>>> >>> sum(tl)
42

# list comprehension = generator expressions wrapped in a list constructor
>>> ml = list( x for x in range(10) )
>>> ml
[0, 1, 2, 3, 4, 5, 6, 7, 8, 9]
```

The major difference between a list comprehension and a generator expression is: while list comprehension produces the entire list, generator expression produces one item at a time.

A generator (or generator expression) is kind of lazy, producing items only when asked for/or when being iterated. For this reason, a generator expression is a much more memory efficient than an equivalent list comprehension.

5.2 Tensor basic

In mathematics, **tensors** are geometric objects that describe linear relations between geometric vectors, scalars, and other tensors. In general, a tensor is a container for data.

In many cases, a tensor could be viewed as a more generalized matrix, but it is not a matrix. So what is the difference?

Both look similar, as any of them could be thought to be containers of data.

It is the **transformation properties** that distinguish a tensor and a matrix. A tensor is a mathematical entity that lives in a structure and interacts with other mathematical entities. If one transforms the other entities in the structure in a regular way, then the tensor must obey a related transformation rule. Thus tensors are dynamic, they will transform when interacting with other mathematical entities. Matrices, on the other hand, don't always have this property.

In pytorch, tensors are similar to NumPy's ndarrays, with the addition being that Tensors can also be used on a GPU to accelerate computing.

If you are familiar with numpy library, you will find that pytorch's tensor has a similar API/member functions as numpy.

Let's look at some solid examples to understand tensor better. I try to list examples with a tensor version, as well as a numpy version.

Warning
Tensorflow/keras may have different tensor API, in the book, I will simply refer to pytorch tensor as tensor.

5.2.1 how to create tensor/NumPy array

- torch.empty: create uninitialized tensor

```
>>> import torch
# create uninitialized 5x3 matrix/tensor
>>> x = torch.empty(5, 3)
>>> x
```

```
tensor([[-2.0446e-35,  4.5793e-41, -2.0446e-35],
        [ 4.5793e-41,  0.0000e+00,  0.0000e+00],
        [ 0.0000e+00,  0.0000e+00,  4.3661e-05],
        [ 8.2990e-33,  1.3563e-19,  1.3563e-19],
        [ 1.7464e-04,  1.3567e-19,  2.4754e-12]])
```

By default, the dtype is float32.

In numpy, we can use np.empty to get similar result:

```
>>> import numpy  as np
>>> b = np.empty( (2,3) )    # uninitialized, output may vary
array([[4.9e-324, 9.9e-324, 1.5e-323],
       [2.0e-323, 2.5e-323, 3.0e-323]])
```

Note the dtype of the created array is float64 in numpy.

The dtype could be different between pytorch and numpy. In this example, torch.empty will use float32 by default, while np.empty is float64 by default. You will see it more clearly when we talk about tensor dtype and numpy ndarray.dtype later.

- torch.rand: construct a randomly initialized tensor:

```
>>> x = torch.rand(5, 3)
>>> x
tensor([[0.3351, 0.6716, 0.5905],
        [0.2403, 0.5610, 0.4237],
        [0.9232, 0.2915, 0.0811],
        [0.6704, 0.5836, 0.1305],
        [0.2371, 0.7002, 0.4933]])
```

In numpy, we can use np.random.rand

```
>>> y = np.random.rand(5,3)
>>> y
array([[0.6920192 , 0.81905014, 0.04997446],
       [0.72517777, 0.06627469, 0.88492223],
```

```
        [0.8745128 , 0.16416619, 0.55487683],
        [0.35716398, 0.86376881, 0.42509621],
        [0.09182396, 0.0770167 , 0.52375001]])
```

- torch.zeros: construct a matrix filled zeros

```
>>> x = torch.zeros(5, 3, dtype=torch.long)
>>> x
tensor([[0, 0, 0],
        [0, 0, 0],
        [0, 0, 0],
        [0, 0, 0],
        [0, 0, 0]])
```

In numpy, we use np.zeros to creates an array full of zeros,

```
>>> b = np.zeros( (2,4) )    # note we pass (2,4) that is the numpy shape
array([[ 0.,   0.,   0.,   0.],
       [ 0.,   0.,   0.,   0.]])
```

- torch.ones: to create a tensor with 1:

```
>>> a = torch.ones(5,3, dtype=torch.int16 )  # dtype can also be specified
>>> a
tensor([[1, 1, 1],
        [1, 1, 1],
        [1, 1, 1],
        [1, 1, 1],
        [1, 1, 1]], dtype=torch.int16)
```

In numpy, we use use np.ones to creates an array full of ones,

```
>>> b= np.ones( (2,3,4), dtype=np.int16 )      # dtype can also be specified
array([[[ 1, 1, 1, 1],
        [ 1, 1, 1, 1],
        [ 1, 1, 1, 1]],
       [[ 1, 1, 1, 1],
        [ 1, 1, 1, 1],
        [ 1, 1, 1, 1]]], dtype=int16)
```

- We can use a normal regular Python list or tuple to create tensor or NumPy array.

```
>>> b = torch.tensor([(1,2,3), (4,5,6), (7,8,9)])
>>> b
tensor([[1, 2, 3],
        [4, 5, 6],
        [7, 8, 9]])
```

In numpy, we can do:

```
>>> b = np.array([(1,2,3), (4,5,6), (7,8,9)])
>>> b
array([[1, 2, 3],
       [4, 5, 6],
       [7, 8, 9]])
```

Numpy array transforms sequences of sequences into two-dimensional arrays, sequences of sequences of sequences into three-dimensional arrays, and so on.

Normally, tensor/numpy will output like this: the last axis is printed from left to right, the second-to-last is printed from top to bottom, the rest are also printed from top to bottom, with each slice separated from the next by an empty line.

5.2.2 convert between tensor and numpy

It is quite easy to convert between torch tensor and numpy array in pytorch.

Please be noted: the Torch Tensor and NumPy array will share their underlying memory locations, and changing one will change the other.

5.2.2.1 numpy(): convert a torch tensor to a numpy array

We can convert a torch tensor to a numpy array using torch tensor's member function numpy().

```
>>> a = torch.ones(5)
# convert to numpy array
>>> b = a.numpy()
# add 1
>>> a.add(1)
>>> a
tensor([1., 1., 1., 1., 1.])
>>> b
[1. 1. 1. 1. 1.]

# add_ means in_place adding 1 ( different from a.add(1) )
>>> a.add_(1)
>>> a
tensor([2., 2., 2., 2., 2.])
# please note the b changed as well
>>> b
[2. 2. 2. 2. 2.]
```

5.2.2.2 from_numpy(): convert numpy array to torch tensor

We can convert a numpy array to torch tensor using torch tensor's member function from_numpy().

```
>>> a = np.ones(5)
>>> b = torch.from_numpy(a)
>>> a
array([1., 1., 1., 1., 1.])
>>> b
tensor([1., 1., 1., 1., 1.], dtype=torch.float64)

# similar to tensor.add(1)
>>> np.add(a, 1)
array([2., 2., 2., 2., 2.])
>>> a
array([1., 1., 1., 1., 1.])
```

```
>>> b
tensor([1., 1., 1., 1., 1.], dtype=torch.float64)


# similar to tensor.add_(1)
>>> np.add(a, 1, out=a)
array([2., 2., 2., 2., 2.])
>>> a
array([2., 2., 2., 2., 2.])
>>> b
tensor([2., 2., 2., 2., 2.], dtype=torch.float64)
```

Note: All the Tensors on the CPU except CharTensor support converting to NumPy and back.

5.2.3 tensor, numpy basic terms

We should know some basic terms in tensor/numpy.

Remember tensor is similar to numpy's ndarray, which is a homogeneous multidimensional array. That means tensor is like numpy **ndarray**, it is a table of elements (usually numbers), all the same type, indexed by a tuple of positive integers.

Maybe it is easier to understand this way: we can treat tensor or numpy.ndarray as of a multidimensional normal python list.

Warning

numpy.array is not the same as the Standard Python Library class array.array, which only handles one-dimensional arrays, and offers less functionality.

In pytorch tensor/NumPy, dimensions are called **axes**. The number of axes is **rank**. For example, the coordinates of a point in 3D space [1, 2, 3] is an array of rank 1. It is not 3 as we normally would say.

Why? Because in tensor/numpy terms, it has only one axis. But that axis has a length of 3, or the size of that axis is 3D.

So when we talk about a point in 3D space in tensor/numpy, it is reduced to one virtual point in one axis. In this way, it is simplified, as it reduces/hides the 3D to 1D dimension.

Tip

See the point? In the world of big data, the less, the better as our brain and intuition work better with lower dimensional data.

Tip

What is **batch axis**? The first axis (axis 0) is called the batch axis or **batch dimension** or **samples axis** as we usually slice data into several batches on the first axis to do the batch training. This is the term we will frequently encounter when using deep-learning libraries.

5.2.3.1 tensor.view or numpy reshape

OK, now, what if we have 100 3D points? How can we represent that? Well, we create 2-dimensional arrays or an array with rank 2.

```
>>> import torch
# split 1,2, ... 300 into 100 part with each as 3D point
# use pytorch build-in function
# by default it is a float32
# range return evenly spaced values within a given interval.
# in our case, it will return one dimension array, 1,2,3, ... 300
# then we use view function to change this array to new shape
>>> a = torch.range(1,300).view(100,3)
>>> a
tensor([[  1.,    2.,    3.],
        [  4.,    5.,    6.],
        ...
        [295., 296., 297.],
        [298., 299., 300.]])
# check the rank or dimension of this tensor
>>> a.dim()
2
```

In numpy, we can do it as:

```
import numpy as np
# split 1,2, ... 300 number into 100 part with each as 3D point
# use NumPy build-in function
# arrange return evenly spaced values within a given interval.
# in our case, it will return one dimension array, 1,2,3, ... 300
# then we use reshape function to change this array to new shape
a = np.arange(300).reshape(100,3)
>>> a
array([[  0,   1,   2],
       [  3,   4,   5],
       [  6,   7,   8],
        ...
       [291, 292, 293],
       [294, 295, 296],
       [297, 298, 299]])
```

Warning

torch.range(a,b) includes both a, b default is float type, while torch.arange(a,b) is similar to numpy.arange(a,b) which does not include b and default data type is int.

5.2.3.2 tensor.dim() or numpy ndarray.ndim

The number of axes (dimensions) of the array. In the Python world, the number of dimensions is referred to as rank.

```
>>> a.dim()
2
>>> a.ndimension()
2
```

If in numpy:

```
>>> a.ndim
2
```

You can see the dimension is 2.

5.2.3.3 tensor.shape or numpy ndarray.shape

This is a tuple of integers showing the size of the array in each dimension/rank.

This is probably one of the most useful and used methods.

In our example:

```
>>> a.shape
torch.Size([100, 3])
```

It means "a" has 100 elements, where each element will have 3-dimensional numbers.

The length of the shape tuple is, therefore, the rank, or the number of dimensions.

In numpy:

```
>>> a.shape
(100, 3)
```

5.2.3.4 tensor.size(), numpy ndarray.size

The total number of elements of the array. This is equal to the product of the elements of shape.

```
>>> a.size()
torch.Size([100, 3])
```

In numpy:

```
>>> a.shape
(100, 3)
```

5.2.3.5 tensor.dtype, numpy ndarray.dtype

It tells us the type of elements in the array.

It can be standard Python types or some torch type: torch.int32, torch.float32 and torch.float64 etc.

```
>>> a.dtype
torch.float32
```

In numpy: It can be standard Python types, or some NumPy type: numpy.int32, numpy.int16, and numpy.float64 etc.

```
>>> a.dtype
dtype('int64')
```

5.2.3.6 tensor.element_size(), numpy ndarray.itemsize

Returns the size in bytes of an individual element.

```
>>> a.element_size()
4
```

In numpy, it refers to the size in bytes of each element of the array. It is equivalent to ndarray.dtype.itemsize.

```
>>> a.itemsize
## int64 mean 64 bits integer, which is 64/8 = 8 bytes
8
```

5.2.3.7 tensor.data or numpy ndarray.data

It is a buffer containing the actual elements of the array. Normally, we won't need to use this attribute because we can access the elements in an array using indexing facilities.

```
>>> a.data
tensor([[  1.,    2.,    3.],
        [  4.,    5.,    6.],
        ...
        ...
        [295., 296., 297.],
        [298., 299., 300.]])
```

In numpy, ndarray.data

```
>>> a.data
array([[  0,    1,    2],
       [  3,    4,    5],
       [  6,    7,    8],
        ...
       [291, 292, 293],
       [294, 295, 296],
       [297, 298, 299]])
```

5.2.4 Tensor/Numpy basic operation

As a general rule, arithmetic operators on tensor/numpy arrays are applied element-wisely.

For example:

```
>>> import torch
>>> a = torch.tensor(  [ [1,1],[2,3] ] )
>>> a
tensor([[1, 1],
        [2, 3]])
>>> b = torch.tensor(  [ (3,4),(5,6) ] )
>>> b
tensor([[3, 4],
        [5, 6]])

# add
>>> c = a + b
```

```
>>> c
tensor([[4, 5],
        [7, 9]])

# multiple
>>> d = a * b
>>> d
tensor([[ 3,  4],
        [10, 18]])

# matrix product/multiple using mm or matmul
>>> torch.mm(a,b)
tensor([[ 8, 10],
        [21, 26]])

>>> a.mm(b)
tensor([[ 8, 10],
        [21, 26]])

>>> a.matmul(b)
tensor([[ 8, 10],
        [21, 26]])

>>> torch.matmul(a,b)
tensor([[ 8, 10],
        [21, 26]])

#torch.dot() means inner product only for 1-D
>>> a.dot(b)
Traceback (most recent call last):
  File "<stdin>", line 1, in <module>
RuntimeError: dot: Expected 1-D argument self, but got 2-D
```

In numpy, we have similar operations:

```
>>> a = np.array( [ [1,1],[2,3] ] )
>>> a
array([[1, 1],
       [2, 3]])
>>> b = np.array( [ [3,4],[5,6] ] )
>>> b
```

```
array([[3, 4],
       [5, 6]])

# add, it will do element wise +
>>> c = a + b
>>> c
array([[4, 5],
       [7, 9]])

# this will do element wise *
>>> a*b
array([[ 3,  4],
       [10, 18]])

# real matrix dot, will need this dot function
>>> a.dot(b)
array([[ 8, 10],
       [21, 26]])

# no np.mm
>>> np.matmul(a,b)
array([[ 8, 10],
       [21, 26]])
```

Warning

torch.dot(), and np.dot() behaves differently.

Specifically, torch.dot() treats both a and b as 1D vectors (irrespective of their original shape) and computes their inner product. For matrix multiplication in PyTorch, use torch.mm(). Numpy's np.dot() in contrast is more flexible; it computes the inner product for 1D arrays and performs matrix multiplication for 2D arrays. More discussion can be found at:
https://github.com/pytorch/pytorch/issues/138

By default, these operations apply to the array as though It was a list of numbers, regardless of its shape. However, by specifying the axis parameter you can apply an operation along the specified axis of an array:

```
>>> b = torch.range(1,12,dtype=torch.int16).view(3,4)
>>>
```

```
>>> b
tensor([[ 1,  2,  3,  4],
        [ 5,  6,  7,  8],
        [ 9, 10, 11, 12]], dtype=torch.int16)
>>> b.sum(dim=0)
tensor([15, 18, 21, 24])
>>> b.sum(dim=1)
tensor([10, 26, 42])
>>> b.min(dim=1)
(tensor([1, 5, 9], dtype=torch.int16), tensor([0, 0, 0]))
>>> b.cumsum(dim=1)
tensor([[ 1,  3,  6, 10],
        [ 5, 11, 18, 26],
        [ 9, 19, 30, 42]])
```

Similarly, in numpy:

```
>>>
>>> b = np.arange(12).reshape(3,4)
>>> b
array([[ 0,  1,  2,  3],
       [ 4,  5,  6,  7],
       [ 8,  9, 10, 11]])
>>>
>>> b.sum(axis=0)                          # sum of each column
array([12, 15, 18, 21])
>>>
>>> b.min(axis=1)                          # min of each row
array([0, 4, 8])
>>>
>>> b.cumsum(axis=1)                       # cumulative sum along each row
array([[ 0,  1,  3,  6],
       [ 4,  9, 15, 22],
       [ 8, 17, 27, 38]])
```

Tip

One way to understand the dimension/axis of tensor/numpy sum is: it collapses the specified dim/axis or index. For example for a tensor with shape (3,4), if we sum up over dim/axis=0, the shape of that new tensor after sum will be (4) if we sum up over dim/axis=1, the shape of that new tensor after sum will be (3) For a tensor with shape (3,2,4), if we sum up over dim/axis=0, the new tensor after sum will be (2,4) if we sum up over dim/axis=1, the new tensor after sum will be (3,4) if we sum up over dim/axis=2, the new tensor after sum will be (3,2).

Beyond 2- or 3-dimensional matrix, it is probably hard to imagine high dimensional those dim/axis, fortunately, most practical problems may just use dim/axis 0 or 1 or 2.

5.2.5 Tensor/Numpy Indexing, Slicing and Iterating

```
>>> a = torch.range(0,9, dtype=torch.int16)**3
>>> a
tensor([ 0,   1,    8,   27,   64,  125,  216,  343,  512,  729],
       dtype=torch.int16)

# from index position 2 to 5
>>> a[2:5]
tensor([8, 27,  64], dtype=torch.int16)

# equivalent to a[0:6:2] = -1000; from start to position 6, exclusive, set every ↩
    2nd element to -1000
>>> a[:6:2] = -1000
>>> a
tensor([-1000,     1, -1000,    27, -1000,   125,   216,   343,   512,   729],
       dtype=torch.int16)

#reverse, not supported ( but works in numpy)
>>> a[ : :-1]
ValueError: negative step not yet supported

#iterating
>>> for i in a:
...     print(i)
tensor(-1000, dtype=torch.int16)
tensor(1, dtype=torch.int16)
tensor(-1000, dtype=torch.int16)
```

```
tensor(27, dtype=torch.int16)
tensor(-1000, dtype=torch.int16)
tensor(125, dtype=torch.int16)
tensor(216, dtype=torch.int16)
tensor(343, dtype=torch.int16)
tensor(512, dtype=torch.int16)
tensor(729, dtype=torch.int16)


>>> b=torch.range(0,23, dtype=torch.int16).reshape(4,3,2)
>>> b
tensor([[[ 0,  1],
         [ 2,  3],
         [ 4,  5]],

        [[ 6,  7],
         [ 8,  9],
         [10, 11]],

        [[12, 13],
         [14, 15],
         [16, 17]],

        [[18, 19],
         [20, 21],
         [22, 23]]], dtype=torch.int16)

>>> b.dim()    # that means we can access element by 3 indexes
3
>>> b.shape  # that means each axis, our index range
torch.Size(4, 3, 2)

>>> b[0]     # the first of element with (3,2) shape
tensor([[0, 1],
        [2, 3],
        [4, 5]], dtype=torch.int16)


>>> b[1]     # the second of element withe (3,2) shape
tensor([[ 6,  7],
        [ 8,  9],
        [10, 11]], dtype=torch.int16)
```

```
>>> b[0][1]
# the first element with (3,2) shape,
# then the second (2:) shape element
tensor([2, 3], dtype=torch.int16)

>>> b[0][0][0]  # access first element
tensor(0, dtype=torch.int16)

#Array Slicing: Accessing Subarrays
# x[start:stop:step]
# If any of these are unspecified,
# they default to the values start=0, stop=size of dimension, step=1.

>>> b[:1]    # first element
tensor([[[0, 1],
         [2, 3],
         [4, 5]]], dtype=torch.int16)

>>> b[-1]    # last element
tensor([[18, 19],
        [20, 21],
        [22, 23]], dtype=torch.int16)

# hard to understand, could think of b[x][y][z]
# while 0:2 means the range 0 <= x < 2
>>> b[0:2,1]      # the first layer's first two element's second element
tensor([[2, 3],
        [8, 9]], dtype=torch.int16)

>>> b[ : ,1]                            # all first layer's element's second element
tensor([[ 2,  3],
        [ 8,  9],
        [14, 15],
        [20, 21]], dtype=torch.int16)

>>> b[1:3]     # the first layer's 1,2 element
tensor([[[ 6,  7],
         [ 8,  9],
         [10, 11]],
```

```
        [[12, 13],
         [14, 15],
         [16, 17]]], dtype=torch.int16)


>>> b[1:3, :]    # same as before
tensor([[[ 6,  7],
         [ 8,  9],
         [10, 11]],

        [[12, 13],
         [14, 15],
         [16, 17]]], dtype=torch.int16)

>>> b[1:3, :, :]  # same as before
tensor([[[ 6,  7],
         [ 8,  9],
         [10, 11]],

        [[12, 13],
         [14, 15],
         [16, 17]]], dtype=torch.int16)
```

Similarly, in numpy:

```
>>> a = np.arange(10)**3
>>> a
array([  0,   1,   8,  27,  64, 125, 216, 343, 512, 729])

# from index position 2 to 5
>>> a[2:5]
array([ 8, 27, 64])

# equivalent to a[0:6:2] = -1000; from start to position 6, exclusive, set every 2nd element to -1000
>>> a[:6:2] = -1000
array([-1000,     1, -1000,    27, -1000,   125,   216,   343,   512,   729])

#reverse, support -1!
>>> a[ : :-1]                                 # reversed a
array([  729,   512,   343,   216,   125, -1000,    27, -1000,     1, -1000])
```

```
>>> for i in a:
...     print(i)

>>> b=np.arange(24).reshape(4,3,2)
>>> b
array([[[ 0,  1],
        [ 2,  3],
        [ 4,  5]],

       [[ 6,  7],
        [ 8,  9],
        [10, 11]],

       [[12, 13],
        [14, 15],
        [16, 17]],

       [[18, 19],
        [20, 21],
        [22, 23]]])
>>> b.ndim   # that means we can access element by 3 indexes
3
>>> b.shape  # that means each axis, our index range
(4, 3, 2)

>>> b[0]    # the first of element with (3,2) shape
array([[0, 1],
       [2, 3],
       [4, 5]])

>>> b[1]    # the second of element withe (3,2) shape
array([[ 6,  7],
       [ 8,  9],
       [10, 11]])

>>> b[0][1]
# the first element with (3,2) shape,
# then the second (2:) shape element
array([2, 3])

>>> b[0][0][0]  # access first element
```

```

#Array Slicing: Accessing Subarrays
# x[start:stop:step]
# If any of these are unspecified,
# they default to the values start=0, stop=size of dimension, step=1.

>>> b[:1]    # first element
array([[[0, 1],
        [2, 3],
        [4, 5]]])
>>> b[-1]    # last element
array([[18, 19],
       [20, 21],
       [22, 23]])

# hard to understand, could think of b[x][y][z]
# while 0:2 means the range 0 <= x < 2
>>> b[0:2,1]      # the first layer's first two element's second element
array([[2, 3],
       [8, 9]])

>>> b[ : ,1]                          # all first layer's element's second element
array([[ 2,  3],
       [ 8,  9],
       [14, 15],
       [20, 21]])

>>> b[1:3]     # the first layer's 1,2 element
array([[[ 6,  7],
        [ 8,  9],
        [10, 11]],

       [[12, 13],
        [14, 15],
        [16, 17]]])

>>> b[1:3, :]    # same as before
array([[[ 6,  7],
        [ 8,  9],
        [10, 11]],

       [[12, 13],
```

```
          [14, 15],
          [16, 17]]])

>>> b[1:3, :, :]  # same as before
array([[[ 6,  7],
          [ 8,  9],
          [10, 11]],

         [[12, 13],
          [14, 15],
          [16, 17]]])
```

5.2.6 Stacking together different tensor/numpy arrays

Several tensors can be stacked together along a different dimension using torch.cat.

```
>>> a = torch.range(0,3).view(2,2)
>>> a
tensor([[0., 1.],
        [2., 3.]])
>>> b = torch.range(4,7).view(2,2)
>>> b
tensor([[4., 5.],
        [6., 7.]])

# stack/concatenate two tensor along axis=0
# similar to numpy.vstack( (a,b) )
>>> torch.cat((a,b), 0)
tensor([[0., 1.],
        [2., 3.],
        [4., 5.],
        [6., 7.]])

# stack/concatenate two tensor along axis=1
>>> similar to  np.hstack((a,b))
>>> torch.cat((a,b), 1)
tensor([[0., 1., 4., 5.],
        [2., 3., 6., 7.]])
```

```
# note: torch.stack is different from torch.cat
>>> torch.stack((a,b), dim=0)
tensor([[[0., 1.],
         [2., 3.]],

        [[4., 5.],
         [6., 7.]]])

>>> torch.stack((a,b), dim=1)
tensor([[[0., 1.],
         [4., 5.]],

        [[2., 3.],
         [6., 7.]]])
```

Warning

torch.cat is different from torch.stack

torch.stack:

Concatenates sequence of tensors along a new dimension. All tensors need to be of the same size.

torch.cat:

Concatenates the given sequence of seq tensors in the given dimension.

All tensors must either have the same shape (except in the concatenating dimension) or be empty. torch.cat() can be seen as an inverse operation for torch.split() and torch.chunk().

Similarly, in numpy: several arrays can be stacked together along a different axis:

```
>>> a=np.arange(0,4).reshape(2,2)
>>> a
array([[0, 1],
       [2, 3]])
>>> b=np.arange(4,8).reshape(2,2)
>>> b
array([[4, 5],
       [6, 7]])
>>> np.vstack( (a,b) )
array([[0, 1],
       [2, 3],
```

```
       [4, 5],
       [6, 7]])
>>> np.hstack( (a,b) )
array([[0, 1, 4, 5],
       [2, 3, 6, 7]])
```

5.2.7 Splitting one tensor/numpy array into several smaller ones

Using **tensor.split**, you can split tensor along its specified axis,

```
>>> a = torch.range(1,72).view(6,12)
>>> a
tensor([[ 1.,  2.,  3.,  4.,  5.,  6.,  7.,  8.,  9., 10., 11., 12.],
        [13., 14., 15., 16., 17., 18., 19., 20., 21., 22., 23., 24.],
        [25., 26., 27., 28., 29., 30., 31., 32., 33., 34., 35., 36.],
        [37., 38., 39., 40., 41., 42., 43., 44., 45., 46., 47., 48.],
        [49., 50., 51., 52., 53., 54., 55., 56., 57., 58., 59., 60.],
        [61., 62., 63., 64., 65., 66., 67., 68., 69., 70., 71., 72.]])

# split the tensor into the size of 2 along dim=0 which is vertical/column
# thinking of dim=0 is the first index of matrix/tensor
>>> b = torch.split(a, 2, dim=0)
>>> b
(tensor([[ 1.,  2.,  3.,  4.,  5.,  6.,  7.,  8.,  9., 10., 11., 12.],
        [13., 14., 15., 16., 17., 18., 19., 20., 21., 22., 23., 24.]]),
 tensor([[25., 26., 27., 28., 29., 30., 31., 32., 33., 34., 35., 36.],
        [37., 38., 39., 40., 41., 42., 43., 44., 45., 46., 47., 48.]]),
 tensor([[49., 50., 51., 52., 53., 54., 55., 56., 57., 58., 59., 60.],
        [61., 62., 63., 64., 65., 66., 67., 68., 69., 70., 71., 72.]]))

# split the tensor into size of 2 along dim=1 which is horizontal/row
# thinking of dim=1 is the second index of matrix/tensor
# similar to np.hsplit(a,6)
>>> c = torch.split(a, 2, dim=1)
>>> c
(tensor([[ 1.,  2.],
        [13., 14.],
        [25., 26.],
        [37., 38.],
```

```
        [49., 50.],
        [61., 62.]]),
 tensor([[ 3.,  4.],
        [15., 16.],
        [27., 28.],
        [39., 40.],
        [51., 52.],
        [63., 64.]]),
 tensor([[ 5.,  6.],
        [17., 18.],
        [29., 30.],
        [41., 42.],
        [53., 54.],
        [65., 66.]]),
 tensor([[ 7.,  8.],
        [19., 20.],
        [31., 32.],
        [43., 44.],
        [55., 56.],
        [67., 68.]]),
 tensor([[ 9., 10.],
        [21., 22.],
        [33., 34.],
        [45., 46.],
        [57., 58.],
        [69., 70.]]),
 tensor([[11., 12.],
        [23., 24.],
        [35., 36.],
        [47., 48.],
        [59., 60.],
        [71., 72.]]))

# split into 2,4 along dim/axis=0
>>> c = torch.split(a, [2,4], dim=0)
>>> c
(tensor([[ 1.,  2.,  3.,  4.,  5.,  6.,  7.,  8.,  9., 10., 11., 12.],
        [13., 14., 15., 16., 17., 18., 19., 20., 21., 22., 23., 24.]]),
 tensor([[25., 26., 27., 28., 29., 30., 31., 32., 33., 34., 35., 36.],
        [37., 38., 39., 40., 41., 42., 43., 44., 45., 46., 47., 48.],
        [49., 50., 51., 52., 53., 54., 55., 56., 57., 58., 59., 60.],
        [61., 62., 63., 64., 65., 66., 67., 68., 69., 70., 71., 72.]]))
```

```
# split into 2,12 along dim/axis=1
>>> d = torch.split(a, [2,10], dim=1)
>>> d
(tensor([[ 1.,  2.],
        [13., 14.],
        [25., 26.],
        [37., 38.],
        [49., 50.],
        [61., 62.]]),
 tensor([[ 3.,  4.,  5.,  6.,  7.,  8.,  9., 10., 11., 12.],
        [15., 16., 17., 18., 19., 20., 21., 22., 23., 24.],
        [27., 28., 29., 30., 31., 32., 33., 34., 35., 36.],
        [39., 40., 41., 42., 43., 44., 45., 46., 47., 48.],
        [51., 52., 53., 54., 55., 56., 57., 58., 59., 60.],
        [63., 64., 65., 66., 67., 68., 69., 70., 71., 72.]]))
```

Similarly in numpy: using **hsplit**, you can split an array along its horizontal axis, either by specifying the number of equally shaped arrays to return, or by specifying the columns after which the division should occur:

```
>>> a
array([[ 1,  2,  3,  4,  5,  6,  7,  8,  9, 10, 11, 12],
       [13, 14, 15, 16, 17, 18, 19, 20, 21, 22, 23, 24],
       [25, 26, 27, 28, 29, 30, 31, 32, 33, 34, 35, 36],
       [37, 38, 39, 40, 41, 42, 43, 44, 45, 46, 47, 48],
       [49, 50, 51, 52, 53, 54, 55, 56, 57, 58, 59, 60],
       [61, 62, 63, 64, 65, 66, 67, 68, 69, 70, 71, 72]])
>>> np.hsplit(a,3)
[array([[ 1,  2,  3,  4],
       [13, 14, 15, 16],
       [25, 26, 27, 28],
       [37, 38, 39, 40],
       [49, 50, 51, 52],
       [61, 62, 63, 64]]), array([[ 5,  6,  7,  8],
       [17, 18, 19, 20],
       [29, 30, 31, 32],
       [41, 42, 43, 44],
       [53, 54, 55, 56],
       [65, 66, 67, 68]]), array([[ 9, 10, 11, 12],
       [21, 22, 23, 24],
       [33, 34, 35, 36],
```

```
        [45, 46, 47, 48],
        [57, 58, 59, 60],
        [69, 70, 71, 72]])]

>>> np.hsplit(a,6)
[array([[ 1,  2],
        [13, 14],
        [25, 26],
        [37, 38],
        [49, 50],
        [61, 62]]),
 array([[ 3,  4],
        [15, 16],
        [27, 28],
        [39, 40],
        [51, 52],
        [63, 64]]),
 array([[ 5,  6],
        [17, 18],
        [29, 30],
        [41, 42],
        [53, 54],
        [65, 66]]),
 array([[ 7,  8],
        [19, 20],
        [31, 32],
        [43, 44],
        [55, 56],
        [67, 68]]),
 array([[ 9, 10],
        [21, 22],
        [33, 34],
        [45, 46],
        [57, 58],
        [69, 70]]),
 array([[11, 12],
        [23, 24],
        [35, 36],
        [47, 48],
        [59, 60],
        [71, 72]])]
```

```
# it is really hard to understand
>>> np.hsplit(a,(3,4))
[array([[ 1,  2,  3],
        [13, 14, 15],
        [25, 26, 27],
        [37, 38, 39],
        [49, 50, 51],
        [61, 62, 63]]),
 array([[ 4],
        [16],
        [28],
        [40],
        [52],
        [64]]),
  array([[ 5,  6,  7,  8,  9, 10, 11, 12],
        [17, 18, 19, 20, 21, 22, 23, 24],
        [29, 30, 31, 32, 33, 34, 35, 36],
        [41, 42, 43, 44, 45, 46, 47, 48],
        [53, 54, 55, 56, 57, 58, 59, 60],
        [65, 66, 67, 68, 69, 70, 71, 72]])]
```

5.2.8 tensor squeeze and unsqueeze

You will see those two functions are invoked a lot in the pytorch code.

The pytorch official document has a good explanation:

```
torch.squeeze will return a tensor with all the dimensions of input of size 1 removed.

For example, if the input is of shape: (A$\times$1$\times$B$\times$C$\times$1$\times$D) then the out tensor will be of shape:
(A$\times$B$\times$C$\times$D).

When dim is given, a squeeze operation is done only in the given dimension.
If the input is of shape: (A$\times$1$\times$B), squeeze(input, 0) leaves the tensor unchanged,
but squeeze(input, 1) will squeeze the tensor to the shape (A$\times$B).
```

The torch.unsqueeze is the opposition operation of torch.squeeze. It returns a new tensor with a dimension of size one inserted at the specified position. The returned tensor shares the same underlying data with this tensor.

The output of torch.unsqueeze is not that obvious. Let's see an example:

```
>>> x = torch.tensor([1, 2, 3, 4])
>>> x.shape
torch.Size([4])

# insert a dimension of size one at index=0
>>> x1 = torch.unsqueeze(x, 0)
tensor([[ 1,  2,  3,  4]])
>>> x1.shape
torch.Size([1, 4])

# insert a dimension of size one at index=1
>>> x2 = torch.unsqueeze(x, 1)
tensor([[ 1],
        [ 2],
        [ 3],
        [ 4]])
>>> x2.shape
torch.Size([4, 1])
```

Both operations (squeeze/unsqueeze) are sort of similar to torch.view, but only focus on the dimension of size one, while torch.view has more flexibility.

5.2.9 tensor contiguous

The concept of contiguous in tensor may be a little confusing.

Some tensor operations (e.g.: narrow(), view(), expand() and transpose()) in PyTorch do not really change the content of the tensor, but only how to convert indices into tensor to byte location.

For example: when you call transpose(), PyTorch doesn't generate new tensor with new layout, it just modifies meta information in Tensor object so offset and stride is for the new shape. The transposed tensor and original tensor shared the same memory, but transposed tensor is not contiguous because because its memory layout is different than a tensor of the same shape made from scratch.

See an example below:

```
>>> x = torch.randn(2, 3)
>>> x tensor([[-0.5593, -0.1294, -0.3254],
        [ 1.2403, -0.2486,  2.1228]])
>>> x.is_contiguous()
True


>>> y = x.transpose(0,1)
>>> y
tensor([[-0.5593,  1.2403],
        [-0.1294, -0.2486],
        [-0.3254,  2.1228]])
>>> y.is_contiguous()
False

# The function torch.contiguous() will make a copy of tensor
# so the order of elements would be same
# as if tensor of the same shape was created from scratch.
>>> y2=y.contiguous()
>>> y2
tensor([[-0.5593,  1.2403],
        [-0.1294, -0.2486],
        [-0.3254,  2.1228]])
>>> y2.is_contiguous()
True
```

5.3 Advanced features provided by Pytorch tensor API

One unique thing of pytorch tensor or a key difference from numpy ndarray is:
pytorch tensor can do automatic differentiation using autograd package.

Quote from pytorch's official tutorial:

https://pytorch.org/tutorials/beginner/blitz/autograd_tutorial.html#sphx-glr-beginner-blitz-autograd-tutorial-py

```
torch.Tensor is the central class of the package.

If you set its attribute .requires_grad as True,
```

```
it tracks all operations on it.
When you finish your computation, you can call .backward()
and have all the gradients computed automatically.
The gradient for this tensor will be accumulated into .grad attribute.

To stop a tensor from tracking history, you can call .detach()
to detach it from the computation history,
and to prevent future computation from being tracked.

To prevent tracking history (and using memory),
you can also wrap the code block in with torch.no_grad():.
This can be particularly helpful when evaluating a model
because the model may have trainable parameters with requires_grad=True,
but for which we don't need the gradients.
```

An example may be better than thousands of words.

The following is an even simpler example than one in the official tutorial. I hope it will help you to understand pytorch's autograd better and quicker.

```
>>> x = torch.ones(2, 2, requires_grad=True)
>>> x
tensor([[1., 1.],
        [1., 1.]], requires_grad=True)

# let's sum x, we got a scalar tensor
>>> z=torch.sum(x)

# Please note we have a gradient function attached to this tensor
>>> z
tensor(4., grad_fn=<SumBackward0>)

# clear the grad result first, you will see
# why we need to do it just a moment
>>> x.grad.data.zero_()

# important!
# most of time our final cost function is a scalar
# since we have a scale tensor,
# we can use backward() without any additional argument
# to calculate delta(z)/delta(x(i)) where i = 0,1,2,3,4
```

```
# obviously it is 1 if you know the calculus.
>>> z.backward()
>>> x.grad
tensor([[1., 1.],
        [1., 1.]])

# do it again, x.grad is accumulated!
# that is why we need to x.grad.data.zero_() before calling backward()
>>> z.backward()
>>> x.grad
tensor([[2., 2.],
        [2., 2.]])
```

I would strongly suggest you read that tutorial online at this time. If you do not quite understand the vector-Jacobian product, hope the following diagram can help you to understand how vector-Jacobian works better.

Let's say we have l is a scalar:

$l = g(\vec{y})$

where :

$\vec{y} = f(\vec{x})$

The gradient of $\vec{y}$ respect to $\vec{x}$ is Jacobian matrix

$$\frac{\partial \vec{y}}{\partial \vec{x}} = J = \begin{pmatrix} \frac{\partial y_1}{\partial x_1} & \cdots & \frac{\partial y_1}{\partial x_n} \\ \cdots & \cdots & \cdots \\ \frac{\partial y_m}{\partial x_1} & \cdots & \frac{\partial y_m}{\partial x_n} \end{pmatrix}$$

the gradient of l respect to $\vec{x}$ is (by the chain rule is:)

$$\frac{\partial l}{\partial \vec{x}} = \frac{\partial l}{\partial \vec{y}} \frac{\partial \vec{y}}{\partial \vec{x}} = \left(\frac{\partial l}{\partial y_1}, \ \ldots, \ \frac{\partial l}{\partial y_m} \right) J$$

If we take the transport on the above equation, we get:

$$\left(\frac{\partial l}{\partial \vec{x}} \right)^T = J^T \begin{pmatrix} \frac{\partial l}{\partial y_1} \\ \cdots \\ \frac{\partial l}{\partial y_m} \end{pmatrix} = J^T v = \begin{pmatrix} \frac{\partial l}{\partial x_1} \\ \cdots \\ \frac{\partial l}{\partial x_n} \end{pmatrix}$$

where

$$v = \begin{pmatrix} \frac{\partial l}{\partial y_1} \\ \cdots \\ \frac{\partial l}{\partial y_m} \end{pmatrix}$$

Figure 5.1: how to calculate the gradient of scalar l w.r.t. x by a chain rule

Remember torch.autograd is an engine for computing vector-Jacobian product, which makes it very convenient to feed external gradients into a model that has non-scalar output.

Chapter 6

Pytorch deep learning basic

With pytorch environment already set up, we should be able to apply pytorch to some toy projects.

Let's start.

6.1 Pytorch's sequential model

If you knew keras, it has a very simple, but powerful sequential model, which makes deep learning easy and fun.

Luckily, Pytorch provides a similar way to define a sequential model.

Here are the high-level steps on how to construct a pytorch's sequential model using pytorch.nn.Sequential.

(1) setup learning model

```
# example to show pytorch's Sequential model
import torch
import torch.nn as nn

# Defining input size, hidden layer size, output size and batch size respectively
n_in, n_h, n_out, batch_size = 100, 64, 10, 32

# Create a model
# keras's dense layer =  nn.Linear + activation function  in pytorch
```

```
model = nn.Sequential(nn.Linear(n_in, n_h),
                      nn.ReLU(),
                      nn.Linear(n_h,n_out))
```

Here we use the torch.nn package to define our model as a sequence of layers: input → linear → relu → linear → output

(2) specify loss/optimizer function for the learning process

Once we set up the model, we need to configure the learning process, e.g.: specify loss function, optimizer for the learning process, etc.

```
# Construct the loss function
criterion = torch.nn.MSELoss(reduction='sum')

# Construct the optimizer (Stochastic Gradient Descent in this case)
optimizer = torch.optim.SGD(model.parameters(), lr=0.01)
```

(3) prepare data

```
# prepare some training data:
# each data point has n_in-dimension input, and n_out-dimension output
num_training = 100
x_train =  torch.FloatTensor(num_training, n_in).uniform_()
y_train =  torch.FloatTensor(num_training, n_out).uniform_()

# prepare validation data
num_val = 10
x_val =  torch.FloatTensor(num_val, n_in).uniform_()
y_val =  torch.FloatTensor(num_val, n_out).uniform_()
```

(4) define a training process

In pytorch, we normally need to define how we train the data.

```
# total epochs
epochs = 5

```

```
4  # when to check the validation
5  N_eval_epoch = 3;
6  
7  # training process, calculate Gradient Descent
8  for epoch in range(epochs):
9      i = 0;
10     print('epoch: ', epoch,' begin .. ')
11     # batch feeding the data
12     for i in range(0, x_train.size()[0], batch_size):
13         # get a batch of data
14         x = x_train[i:i+batch_size]
15         y = y_train[i:i+batch_size]
16 
17         # Forward pass: Compute predicted y by passing x to the model
18         y_pred = model(x)
19 
20         # Compute and print loss
21         loss = criterion(y_pred, y)
22         print('i: ', i,' loss: ', loss.item())
23 
24         # Zero gradients, perform a backward pass and update the weights.
25         optimizer.zero_grad()
26 
27         # perform a backward pass (backpropagation)
28         loss.backward()
29 
30         # Update the parameters
31         optimizer.step()
```

- Line 11-14, we get a batch_size of data,
- Line 17, we predicted y by passing x to the model.
- Line 20, we calculate the loss.
- Line 25 - 31, we do the backpropagation then update the parameters. Be noted, before the backward pass, we need to use the optimizer object to zero all of the gradients for the variables it will update (which are the learnable weights of the model). This is because by default gradients are accumulated in tensor's grad, please check tensor.autograd in the last chapter.

Warning

In Keras, such code is not needed. This could be seen as one of the cons in Pytorch. But on the positive side, it gives users a lot of flexibility to customize the training procedure.

(5) define a validation process

Generally, we also need to evaluate the model's performance using the validation set.

Here is the code:

```
1       # Validation
2       if epoch%N_eval_epoch==0:
3         with torch.no_grad():
4           for i in range(0, x_test.size()[0], batch_size):
5             x = x_test[i:i+batch_size]
6             y = y_test[i:i+batch_size]
7             y_pred = model(x)
8             if torch.equal( y, y_pred ):
9               print("validation: predict correct")
10            else:
11              print("validation: predict wrong")
```

Note in Line 3, since we are inside an evaluation process, we do not need to do any backpropagation, thus we can stop autograd from tracking history on Tensors(with .requires_grad=True) by wrapping the code block in with torch.no_grad().

(5) predict the data

Once we are satisfied with the model, we can use it to predict:

```
y_pred = model(x_test)
```

Tip

You can download the complete code of this example from the author's repo (https://github.com/mingewang/pytorch_deep_learning_by_example) at: basic/seq_model_example.py

6.2 Pytorch's powerful custom module model

Many times we may need to specify more complex models than just a sequence/combination of existing modules.

Pytorch provides a way to do that, it is similar to keras's functional API model, but maybe even more flexible.

What we need to do is:
first, define our own Modules by subclassing nn.Module,
then define a forward function, which receives input Tensors and produces output Tensors using other modules or any other autograd operations on Tensors.

The previous example can be re-written as:

```
# example to show pytorch's custom model
import torch
import torch.nn as nn

class MyNet(torch.nn.Module):
  def __init__(self, n_in, n_h, n_out):
    """
    In the constructor we instantiate two nn.Linear modules and assign them as
    member variables.
    """
    super(MyNet, self).__init__()
    self.linear1 = torch.nn.Linear(n_in, n_h)
    self.linear2 = torch.nn.Linear(n_h, n_out)

  def forward(self, x):
    """
    In the forward function we accept a Tensor of input data and we must return
    a Tensor of output data. We can use Modules defined in the constructor as
    well as arbitrary operators on Tensors.
    """
    h_relu = self.linear1(x).clamp(min=0)
    y_pred = self.linear2(h_relu)
    return y_pred


# Defining input size, hidden layer size, output size and batch size respectively
n_in, n_h, n_out, batch_size = 100, 64, 10, 32

```

```
# Create a model
model = MyNet(n_in, n_h, n_out)

# Construct the loss function
criterion = torch.nn.MSELoss(reduction='sum')

# Construct the optimizer (Stochastic Gradient Descent in this case)
optimizer = torch.optim.SGD(model.parameters(), lr=0.01)

# prepare some data:
# each data point has n_in-dimension input, and n_out-dimension output
num_training = 100
x_train =  torch.FloatTensor(num_training, n_in).uniform_()
y_train =  torch.FloatTensor(num_training, n_out).uniform_()

num_val = 10
x_val =  torch.FloatTensor(num_val, n_in).uniform_()
y_val =  torch.FloatTensor(num_val, n_out).uniform_()

epochs = 5

# when to check the validation
N_eval_epoch = 3;

# training process, calculate Gradient Descent
for epoch in range(epochs):
    i = 0;
    print('epoch: ', epoch,' begin .. ')
    # batch feeding the data
    for i in range(0, x_train.size()[0], batch_size):
      # get a batch of data
      x = x_train[i:i+batch_size]
      y = y_train[i:i+batch_size]

      # Forward pass: Compute predicted y by passing x to the model
      y_pred = model(x)

      # Compute and print loss
      loss = criterion(y_pred, y)
      print('i: ', i,' loss: ', loss.item())

      # Zero gradients, perform a backward pass, and update the weights.
```

```
        optimizer.zero_grad()

        # perform a backward pass (backpropagation)
        loss.backward()

        # Update the parameters
        optimizer.step()

    # Validation
    if epoch%N_eval_epoch==0:
        with torch.no_grad():
            for i in range(0, x_val.size()[0], batch_size):
                x = x_val[i:i+batch_size]
                y = y_val[i:i+batch_size]
                y_pred = model(x)
                if torch.equal( y, y_pred ):
                    print("validation: predict correct")
                else:
                    print("validation: predict wrong")
```

As you see, it is almost the same as the sequential model. The major difference is how we define our own module. In many cases, we just need to define:

- a ***init*** function, which defines what modules we want to include.
- a **forward function**, which defines how we want to process the input data, We can use Modules defined in the constructor as well as arbitrary operators on Tensor.
- torch.nn.Module has a default **backward function**, which update the parameters during the backward phase. Normally we just use that default built-in function. But potentially, you can overwrite the default backward function with your own backward function as shown below:

```
def backward(self, input):
    # here you call the function!
    output = my_function(input, self.parameters)
    return output
```

Tip

You can download the complete code of this example from the author's repo (https://github.com/mingewang/pytorch_deep_learning_by_example) at: basic/cus_model_example.py

As you can see, it is much more flexible than the sequential model!

Actually, many projects in pytorch use this style to set up a deep learning model.

6.3 how to debug pytorch using pdb

Easy debugging is one of the main advantages of pytorch. We can insert a breakpoint at any point using: pdb.set_trace()

See below:

```
# debug_example.py
import torch
import torch.nn as nn

class MyNet(torch.nn.Module):
  def __init__(self, n_in, n_h, n_out):
    super(MyNet, self).__init__()
    self.linear1 = torch.nn.Linear(n_in, n_h)
    self.linear2 = torch.nn.Linear(n_h, n_out)
    import pdb
    pdb.set_trace()

  def forward(self, x):
    h_relu = self.linear1(x).clamp(min=0)
    y_pred = self.linear2(h_relu)
    return y_pred

n_in, n_h, n_out, batch_size = 100, 64, 10, 32

model = MyNet(n_in, n_h, n_out)
```

Just run the code, python will drop you into a pdb (python debugger) prompt. You should see the output similar to the following:

```
 python debug_example.py
--Return--
> basic/debug_example.py(10)__init__()->None
-> pdb.set_trace()
(Pdb) l
  5         def __init__(self, n_in, n_h, n_out):
  6           super(MyNet, self).__init__()
  7           self.linear1 = torch.nn.Linear(n_in, n_h)
  8           self.linear2 = torch.nn.Linear(n_h, n_out)
  9           import pdb
 10  ->       pdb.set_trace()
 11
 12         def forward(self, x):
 13           h_relu = self.linear1(x).clamp(min=0)
 14           y_pred = self.linear2(h_relu)
 15           return y_pred
(Pdb) p self
MyNet(
  (linear1): Linear(in_features=100, out_features=64, bias=True)
  (linear2): Linear(in_features=64, out_features=10, bias=True)
)
(Pdb) ?

Documented commands (type help <topic>):
========================================
EOF    c          d        h         list      q        rv       undisplay
a      cl         debug    help      ll        quit     s        unt
alias  clear      disable  ignore    longlist  r        source   until
args   commands   display  interact  n         restart  step     up
b      condition  down     j         next      return   tbreak   w
break  cont       enable   jump      p         retval   u        whatis
bt     continue   exit     l         pp        run      unalias  where

Miscellaneous help topics:
==========================
exec  pdb

(Pdb) c
```

Tip

You can download the complete code of this example from the author's repo (https://github.com/mingewang/pytorch_deep_learning_by_example) at: basic/debug_example.py

More document about pdb can be found at:

https://docs.python.org/3/library/pdb.html

6.4 summary

After reading this chapter, you should know:

- how to use a sequential model to create DNN in pytorch.
- how to write a custom module to create a pytorch DNN model.
- how to debug pytorch using pdb.

Chapter 7

MNIST CNN example: A deep dive of how to handle image data

With all the knowledge learned from previous chapters, now we have the capabilities to tackle real deep learning problems.

Pytorch git repository includes many great examples:

https://github.com/pytorch/examples

We can learn much faster by reading those excellent examples.

Let's first look at a famous MNIST CNN example due to its simplicity. It is essentially a "Hello World" in deep learning.

We will spend a lot of effort to walk through almost every detail from this example. Hopefully, it will show you all the aspects of how a real deep learning problem is solved in pytorch.

Important
If this is the first time you touch deep learning, I would suggest you follow this chapter step by step carefully. Because this chapter will cover many basic, common deep learning/pytroch concepts/techniques, which could be applied to many other ML problems.

7.1 What's MNIST?

The **MNIST** database (Modified National Institute of Standards and Technology database) is a large database of handwritten digits that is commonly used for training various image processing systems.

Please see some examples below:

Figure 7.1: MNIST sample images

The dataset includes not only images of handwritten digits, but also their associated labels.

It is a relatively small dataset in the big-data era, thus is widely used for a demo.

Usually, people split the dataset into three parts: 55,000 data points of training data (mnist.train), 5,000 points of validation data (mnist.validation). 10,000 points of test data (mnist.test),

You can read more detailed background information at:

https://www.tensorflow.org/versions/r1.1/get_started/mnist/beginners

https://elitedatascience.com/keras-tutorial-deep-learning-in-python#step-4

In this chapter, what we will show is:

- how to use pytorch to build a model.
- how to train the model using MNIST dataset.
- how to predict a digit from a new handwritten image.

7.2 MNIST CNN error rate

Let's first quickly run mnist_cnn.py from https://github.com/mingewang/pytorch_deep_learning_by_example/, you should see something similar to:

```
# clone pytorch git repo
git clone https://github.com/mingewang/pytorch_deep_learning_by_example/
cd basic

python mnist.py
Downloading http://yann.lecun.com/exdb/mnist/train-images-idx3-ubyte.gz
Downloading http://yann.lecun.com/exdb/mnist/train-labels-idx1-ubyte.gz
Downloading http://yann.lecun.com/exdb/mnist/t10k-images-idx3-ubyte.gz
Downloading http://yann.lecun.com/exdb/mnist/t10k-labels-idx1-ubyte.gz
Processing...
Done!
Train Epoch: 1 [0/60000 (0%)]   Loss: 2.300039
Train Epoch: 1 [640/60000 (1%)] Loss: 2.213460
Train Epoch: 1 [1280/60000 (2%)]        Loss: 2.170403
...
Train Epoch: 1 [58880/60000 (98%)]      Loss: 0.206954
Train Epoch: 1 [59520/60000 (99%)]      Loss: 0.063979

Test set: Average loss: 0.1019, Accuracy: 9665/10000 (97%)

Train Epoch: 2 [0/60000 (0%)]   Loss: 0.145472
Train Epoch: 2 [640/60000 (1%)] Loss: 0.120431
Train Epoch: 2 [1280/60000 (2%)]        Loss: 0.102170
...
...
Train Epoch: 10 [58240/60000 (97%)]     Loss: 0.164183
Train Epoch: 10 [58880/60000 (98%)]     Loss: 0.006053
Train Epoch: 10 [59520/60000 (99%)]     Loss: 0.007631

Test set: Average loss: 0.0319, Accuracy: 9895/10000 (99%)
```

The accuracy is 0.99, which means the error rate is 1%, which is not bad.

BTW, the best error rate so far is 0.21%, published in Nov 2016 by Romanuke, Vadim who used 5 6-layers' convolutional neural networks.

7.3 MNIST CNN source code

Now let's look at the code:

```
from __future__ import print_function
import argparse
import torch
import torch.nn as nn
import torch.nn.functional as F
import torch.optim as optim
from torchvision import datasets, transforms


class Net(nn.Module):
    def __init__(self):
        super(Net, self).__init__()
        self.conv1 = nn.Conv2d(1, 20, 5, 1)
        self.conv2 = nn.Conv2d(20, 50, 5, 1)
        self.fc1 = nn.Linear(4*4*50, 500)
        self.fc2 = nn.Linear(500, 10)

    def forward(self, x):
        x = F.relu(self.conv1(x))
        x = F.max_pool2d(x, 2, 2)
        x = F.relu(self.conv2(x))
        x = F.max_pool2d(x, 2, 2)
        x = x.view(-1, 4*4*50)
        x = F.relu(self.fc1(x))
        x = self.fc2(x)
        return F.log_softmax(x, dim=1)

def train(args, model, device, train_loader, optimizer, epoch):
    model.train()
    for batch_idx, (data, target) in enumerate(train_loader):
        data, target = data.to(device), target.to(device)
        optimizer.zero_grad()
        output = model(data)
        loss = F.nll_loss(output, target)
        loss.backward()
        optimizer.step()
```

```
        if batch_idx % args.log_interval == 0:
            print('Train Epoch: {} [{}/{} ({:.0f}%)]\tLoss: {:.6f}'.format(
                epoch, batch_idx * len(data), len(train_loader.dataset),
                100. * batch_idx / len(train_loader), loss.item()))

def test(args, model, device, test_loader):
    model.eval()
    test_loss = 0
    correct = 0
    with torch.no_grad():
        for data, target in test_loader:
            data, target = data.to(device), target.to(device)
            output = model(data)
            test_loss += F.nll_loss(output, target, reduction='sum').item() # sum up batch loss
            pred = output.argmax(dim=1, keepdim=True) # get the index of the max log-probability
            correct += pred.eq(target.view_as(pred)).sum().item()

    test_loss /= len(test_loader.dataset)

    print('\nTest set: Average loss: {:.4f}, Accuracy: {}/{} ({:.0f}%)\n'.format(
        test_loss, correct, len(test_loader.dataset),
        100. * correct / len(test_loader.dataset)))

def main():
    # Training settings
    parser = argparse.ArgumentParser(description='PyTorch MNIST Example')
    parser.add_argument('--batch-size', type=int, default=64, metavar='N',
                        help='input batch size for training (default: 64)')
    parser.add_argument('--test-batch-size', type=int, default=1000, metavar='N',
                        help='input batch size for testing (default: 1000)')
    parser.add_argument('--epochs', type=int, default=10, metavar='N',
                        help='number of epochs to train (default: 10)')
    parser.add_argument('--lr', type=float, default=0.01, metavar='LR',
                        help='learning rate (default: 0.01)')
    parser.add_argument('--momentum', type=float, default=0.5, metavar='M',
                        help='SGD momentum (default: 0.5)')
    parser.add_argument('--no-cuda', action='store_true', default=False,
                        help='disables CUDA training')
    parser.add_argument('--seed', type=int, default=1, metavar='S',
                        help='random seed (default: 1)')
```

```
    parser.add_argument('--log-interval', type=int, default=10, metavar='N',
                        help='how many batches to wait before logging training ↩
                            status')

    parser.add_argument('--save-model', action='store_true', default=False,
                        help='For Saving the current Model')
    args = parser.parse_args()
    use_cuda = not args.no_cuda and torch.cuda.is_available()

    torch.manual_seed(args.seed)

    device = torch.device("cuda" if use_cuda else "cpu")

    kwargs = {'num_workers': 1, 'pin_memory': True} if use_cuda else {}
    train_loader = torch.utils.data.DataLoader(
        datasets.MNIST('../data', train=True, download=True,
                       transform=transforms.Compose([
                           transforms.ToTensor(),
                           transforms.Normalize((0.1307,), (0.3081,))
                       ])),
        batch_size=args.batch_size, shuffle=True, **kwargs)
    test_loader = torch.utils.data.DataLoader(
        datasets.MNIST('../data', train=False, transform=transforms.Compose([
                           transforms.ToTensor(),
                           transforms.Normalize((0.1307,), (0.3081,))
                       ])),
        batch_size=args.test_batch_size, shuffle=True, **kwargs)


    model = Net().to(device)
    optimizer = optim.SGD(model.parameters(), lr=args.lr, momentum=args.momentum)

    for epoch in range(1, args.epochs + 1):
        train(args, model, device, train_loader, optimizer, epoch)
        test(args, model, device, test_loader)

    if (args.save_model):
        torch.save(model.state_dict(),"mnist_cnn.pt")

if __name__ == '__main__':
    main()
```

Tip

In order to understand the code more effectively, I suggest you make a copy of this code, or read the code on a computer while reading the book. The code is at:
https://github.com/mingewang/pytorch_deep_learning_by_example/blob/master/basic/mnist.py

7.4 MNIST DNN architecture

- Line 10 - 26, defined a python class to specify DNN architecture for this problem.
- Line 11 - 16, declared all the layers we want to use in the constructor.
- Line 18 - 26, to understand this DNN, we need to look at: forward() function inside this class. The forward() function defines how a model processes the input data, eventually what is the output.
  In this example, the input (MNIST) image will be passed to a 2d convolution layer (conv1), then a relu will be applied on that output (Line 19). The following figure show it clearly:

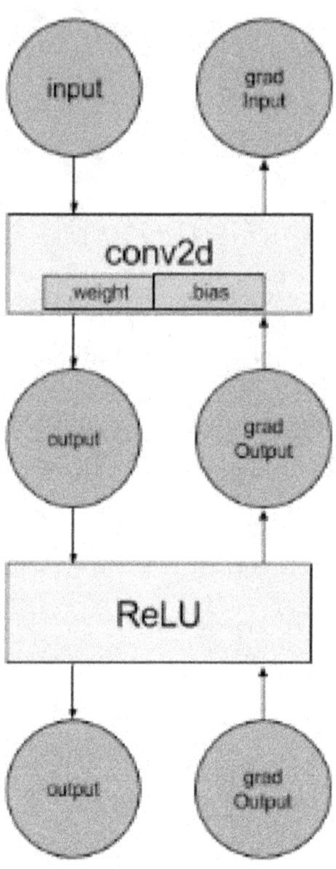

Figure 7.2: conv2d and relu

After that, we will apply a max_pool2d operation (Line 20), pass the result to the second convolution layer (conv2), and apply relu (Line 21).

In Line 22, we apply another max_pool2d operation.

Then we reshape the output (Line 23), feed it into a linear layer, with another relu operation (Line 24).

Finally, we feed the data into another linear layer (Line 25), apply log_softmax.

To understand this architecture, let's dig into those layers for more details.

7.4.1 Conv1d, Conv2d, Conv3d

If you look at pytorch document:

https://pytorch.org/docs/stable/nn.html#convolution-layers

There are Conv1d, Conv2d, Conv3d etc.
What are the differences? Why do we choose Conv2d here?

Well, all those convolutional layers apply sliding convolutional filters to the input.

The following diagrams will give you more details:

(1) Conv1d

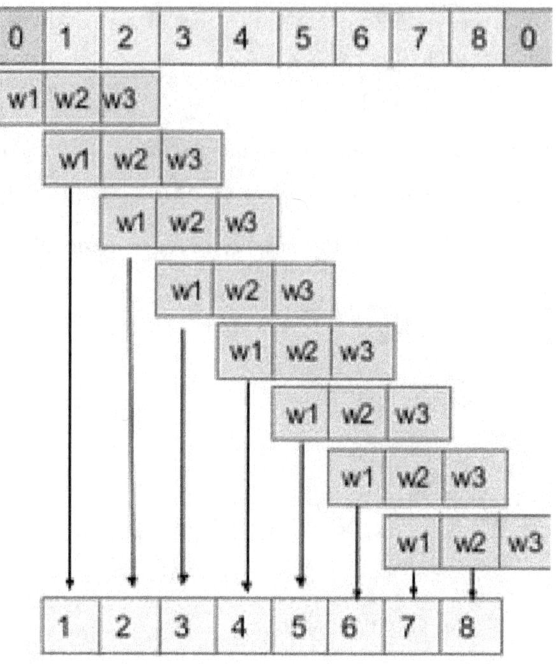

Figure 7.3: Conv1d operation on 1-d sequence text

Conv1d layer convolves the input by moving the filters along 1 direction, (e.g. time-axis or x-axis), then computing the dot product of the weights and the input. e.g.: we can calculate temporal convolution on time-serial data. Anyway, it could be used to process sequence dataset.

(2) Conv2d

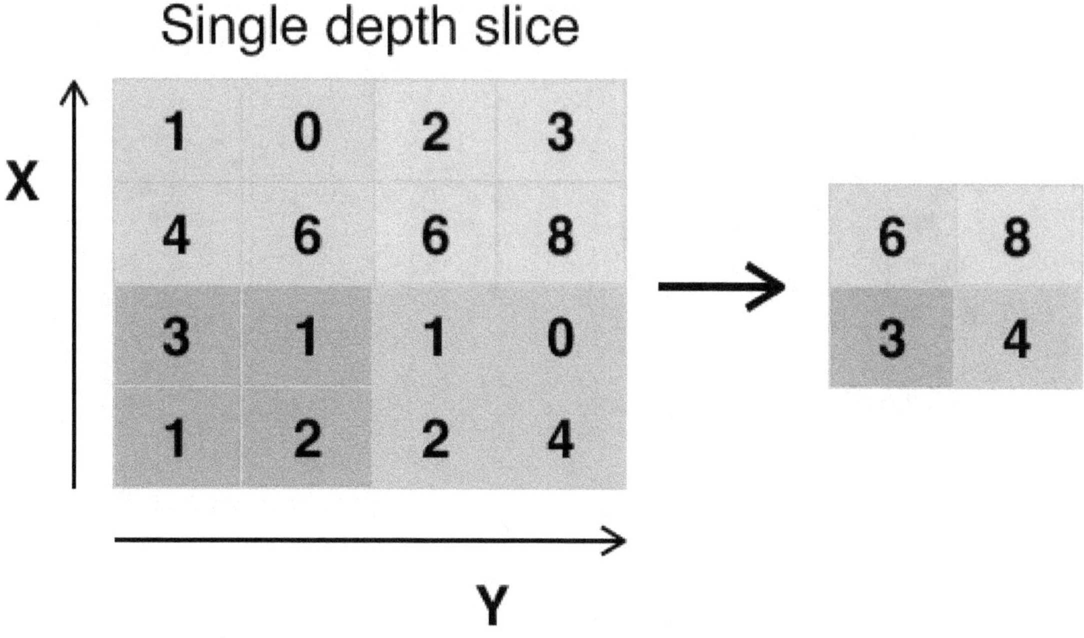

Figure 7.4: Conv2d operation on 2-d image

Conv2d layer convolves by moving 2 directions, e.g.: (x,y) vertically and horizontally in 2-D space. e.g.: we can apply spatial convolution over images. Conv2d is usually used for image processing.

(3) Conv3d

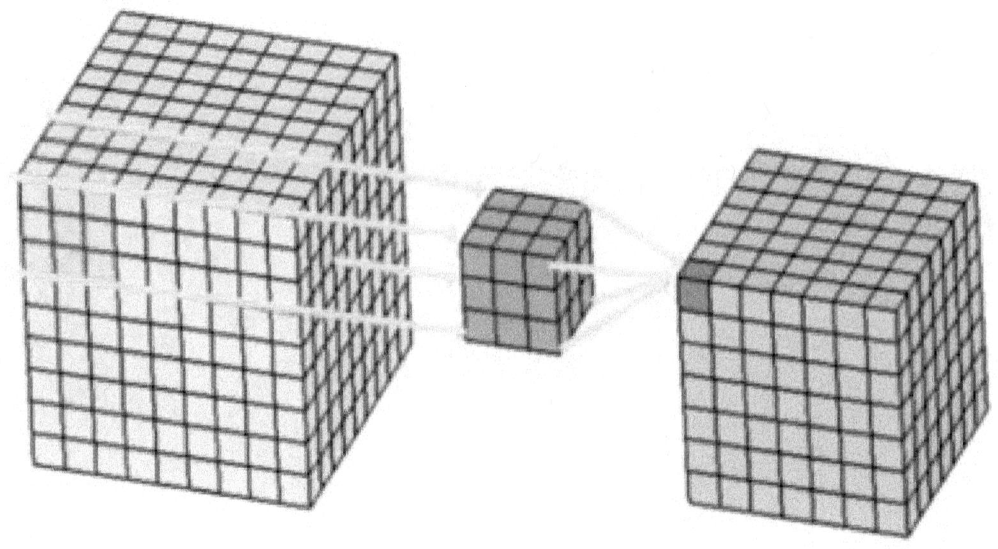

Figure 7.5: Conv3d operation on 3-d image

Conv3d layer convolves by moving in 3 directions, e.g.: spatial convolution over volumes, (x,y,z) in 3-D spaces. For example, to handle videos, 3D medical images etc, we can use Conv3d.

As you can image, theoretically, we can define **Conv4d** layer or any higher dimensional convolution layer.

7.4.2 How to use conv2d API

In this example, as MNIST data are images, we will use Conv2d.

At line 13,14, we pass some parameters to Conv2d. What are those magic parameters?

Pytorch document (https://pytorch.org/docs/stable/nn.html#conv2d) says:

```
torch.nn.Conv2d(in_channels, out_channels, kernel_size, stride=1, padding=0,
dilation=1, groups=1, bias=True)

in_channels (int) - Number of channels in the input image
```

```
out_channels (int) - Number of channels produced by the convolution
kernel_size (int or tuple) - Size of the convolving kernel
stride (int or tuple, optional) - Stride of the convolution. Default: 1
padding (int or tuple, optional) - Zero-padding added to both sides of the input. Default: 0
dilation (int or tuple, optional) - Spacing between kernel elements. Default: 1
groups (int, optional) - Number of blocked connections from input channels to output channels. Default: 1
bias (bool, optional) - If True, adds a learnable bias to the output. Default: True
```

So "nn.Conv2d(1, 20, 5, 1)" (Line 13) means: we set up a conv2d layer with 1 channel in the input image (that means the color info is just grey-scale), and we output 20 channels after the convolution, (usually, it means we will apply 20 filters), where the convolution kernel size is 5x5 (a single integer to specify the same value for all spatial dimensions), and stride is 1.

The same applies to line 14 nn.Conv2d(20, 50, 5, 1), we take 20 channels image data which was output from the last layer, then output a 50 channels after the convolution, with kernel size: 5x5, and stride: 1.

Let's look at an example by feeding an image with height h, and width w:

```
>>> import torch
>>> import torch.nn as nn
>>> m = nn.Conv2d(1, 20, 5, 1)

# our input is 10 batches of 1 channel image data with height 28, and width 28
>>> input = torch.randn(10, 1, 28, 28)

# now pass to our Conv2d
>>> output = m(input)

# we get some output, shape is:
>>> output.shape
torch.Size([10, 20, 24, 24])
```

We got 10 batches of 20 channels image data with 24x24 as height and width. Hmmm, why is the output image 24x24 instead of 28x28?

Well, that is the nature of convolution, the output will get smaller as we slide the kernel window over the image.

Actually pytorch gives us a nice document on how to calculate the new height and width:

Shape:

- Input: $(N, C_{in}, H_{in}, W_{in})$
- Output: $(N, C_{out}, H_{out}, W_{out})$ where

$$H_{out} = \left\lfloor \frac{H_{in} + 2 \times \text{padding}[0] - \text{dilation}[0] \times (\text{kernel\_size}[0] - 1) - 1}{\text{stride}[0]} + 1 \right\rfloor$$

$$W_{out} = \left\lfloor \frac{W_{in} + 2 \times \text{padding}[1] - \text{dilation}[1] \times (\text{kernel\_size}[1] - 1) - 1}{\text{stride}[1]} + 1 \right\rfloor$$

Variables:

- **weight** (*Tensor*) – the learnable weights of the module of shape (out_channels, in_channels, kernel_size[0], kernel_size[1]). The values of these weights are sampled from $\mathcal{U}(-\sqrt{k}, \sqrt{k})$ where $k = \frac{1}{C_{\text{in}} * \prod_{i=0}^{1} \text{kernel\_size}[i]}$
- **bias** (*Tensor*) – the learnable bias of the module of shape (out_channels). If `bias` is `True`, then the values of these weights are sampled from $\mathcal{U}(-\sqrt{k}, \sqrt{k})$ where $k = \frac{1}{C_{\text{in}} * \prod_{i=0}^{1} \text{kernel\_size}[i]}$

Figure 7.6: conv2d input shape ⇒ output shape

An input of (N,C,H,W) means N batches of image data and every batch of image data has C in_channels with height of H and width of W.

If we put the number into those equations, we got exactly the same 24x24 as the output image's height and width.

Now let's try to understand the code with more details.

Here we have 1x28x28 images, we will use Conv2D to process the data.

The kernel_size=(5,5) tells pytorch to use 5x5 kernel, there will be 25 elements in that kernel/matrix.

If we allow only (0,1) in the filter, we could have 2^{25} = 33554432 different kinds of filters. That means this kernel could recognize 33554432 patterns.

But we do not want to use all those 33554432 filters, that can be limited by the out_channels parameter.

Actually, we can put any real number (not just 0/1) in that filter, so patterns it can be recognized is unlimited.

In this example, we tell pytorch to use 20 different filters to do the convolution.

For each filter in the first layer, we transform the image from 28 x 28 to 24x24 with 20 different filters, thus we will get 24x24x20 data points after convolution. Then we apply relu activation to that data (Line 19).

Line 14 adds another Conv2D, but this time, it is only 50 5x5 filters Why? Well, ML tells us each layer learns different things. The intuition is: we want to recognize 20 basic patterns (e.g. edges) in the first layer, then recognize 50 patterns (e.g. textures based on edges pattern from the first layer) in the second layer. The number of texture patterns may be more than the number of edge patterns.

We can stack up more Conv2D layers. But how many layers do we want? That is actually a **black art** in deep learning. We do not know; we have to either based on our experiences or to use trial and error method to find a reasonably good architecture.

7.4.3 max_pool2d function, pooling layer

In Line 20 and Line 22, we applied **maxpool2d** operation to the relu output data, or we can view this as adding a max pool layer.

That means we just get the max value from a 2x2 area. It can reduce data points, thus reducing the computing cost.

Here we used a function (torch.nn.functional.max_pool2d) instead of max pool module (torch.nn.MaxPool2d). They provide essentially the same thing.

There are many other types of pooling operations, more documents can be found at:

https://pytorch.org/docs/stable/nn.html#pooling-layers

https://pytorch.org/docs/stable/_modules/torch/nn/functional.html

7.4.4 Flatten layer or reshape

Line 23, we reshape the data to shape: (batch_size, 4*4*50)

It flattens the input, but does not affect the batch size.

Why 4*4*50?

Let's look at an input with a shape of: 28*28*1, remember relu does NOT change the shape, so after line 19, conv2d(1,20, 5, 1), it become : 24 * 24 * 20 after line 20, max_pool2d(2x2), it becomes: 12 * 12 * 20 after line 21, the second conv2d(20,50,5,1), it becomes: 8*8*50 finally line 22, after max_pool2d(2x2), it becomes: 4 * 4 * 50

This is how we get the output with the shape of 4*4*50.

Instead of hard code the magic number 4*4*50, probably it is probably better to use a flatten module. Pytorch does not provide a built-in flatten module but it is easy to write our own flatten module:

```
# flatten module
class Flatten(nn.Module):

    def __init__(self):
        super(Flatten, self).__init__()

    def forward(self, x):
        shape = torch.prod(torch.tensor(x.shape[1:])).item()
        return x.view(-1, shape)

# e.g. how to use it
flat=Flatten()
x = flat(x)
```

You may ask why do we want to flatten the input?

Well, the last stage/component/layer of CNN is a typical ANN (artificial neural network) classifier, which is often composed by a **fully connected layer** (also called **dense layer**) and softmax layer.

Tip

The dense layer sometimes is also a called connectionist systems due to its highly interconnected, neuron-like processing units.

Just like any classifier, an ANN classifier needs individual features in order to complete a classification task. This means it needs a **feature vector** as an input here.

Therefore, we convert the output from the convolutional part of the CNN into a 1D feature vector, which can then be used by the ANN classifier. This operation is called **flattening**. In other word, it simply gets the output of the convolutional layers, flattens all its structure to create a single long feature vector, then feed into the dense layer/softmax for the final classification.

7.4.5 Linear layer + activation (dense layer)

In pytorch, one of the basic building blocks of deep networks are of the form:

Linear layer + Point-wise nonlinearity / activation.

Keras rolls these two into one, called **dense layer**.

The linear layer applies a linear transformation to input data:

```
torch.nn.Linear(in_features, out_features, bias=True)

Parameters:
in_features - size of each input sample
out_features - size of each output sample
bias - If set to False, the layer will not learn an additive bias. Default: True
```

Line 24 adds a linear layer with activation of ReLu function. We collapse a 4*4*50-dim input to 500-dim outputs.

Line 25 adds a linear layer with no activation function, but collapse 500-dim into 10 outputs, thus we can classify 10 digits.

In Line 26, we calculate log_softmax on that 10 outputs. Why do we have dim=1 in that function: F.log_softmax(x, dim=1)? Remember the output from Line 25 has a shape of (batch_size, 10), we just need to calculate softmax on data along the second axis.

For classification problems, we usually use softmax at the last layer.

More details about linear layer can be found at:

https://pytorch.org/docs/stable/nn.html#linear-layers

7.5 MNIST data, dataset, dataloader

Before training, we need to know how to load data in pytorch.

From high level point of view, a pytorch system will need to use torch.utils.data.DataLoader to load a pytorch dataset.

Warning

If you are from keras/tensorflow background, pytorch's procedure to load data is totally different from them.

Let's look at what is pytorch dataset (will refer as dataset later) first.

7.5.1 Dataset class

torch.utils.data.Dataset is an abstract class representing a **dataset**.

Our custom dataset should inherit Dataset and override the following methods:

- "__len__", for example, len(dataset) returns the size of the dataset.
- "__getitem__" should support the indexing, such that dataset[i] can be used to get ith sample.

For this MNIST dataset, pytorch has already provided an dataset implementation. You can find it at:

https://pytorch.org/docs/1.0.0/_modules/torchvision/datasets/mnist.html

In the following code, we can just use "*len*", and "*getitem*" to explore this dataset.

```
>>> import torch
>>> from torchvision import datasets, transforms
>>> import matplotlib.pyplot as plt
>>> data_dir="../data"
>>> training_ds = datasets.MNIST(data_dir,train=True, download=True)

>>> training_ds.__len__()
60000

# Let's get the first image
>>> img1=training_ds.__getitem__(0)
>>> img1
(<PIL.Image.Image image mode=L size=28x28 at 0x7F0FD3D64390>, tensor(5))

# image height, width (size)
>>> img1.size
(28, 28)

# img1[0] is the image of digit 5, img1[1] is label 5
>>>plt.imshow(img1[0])
```

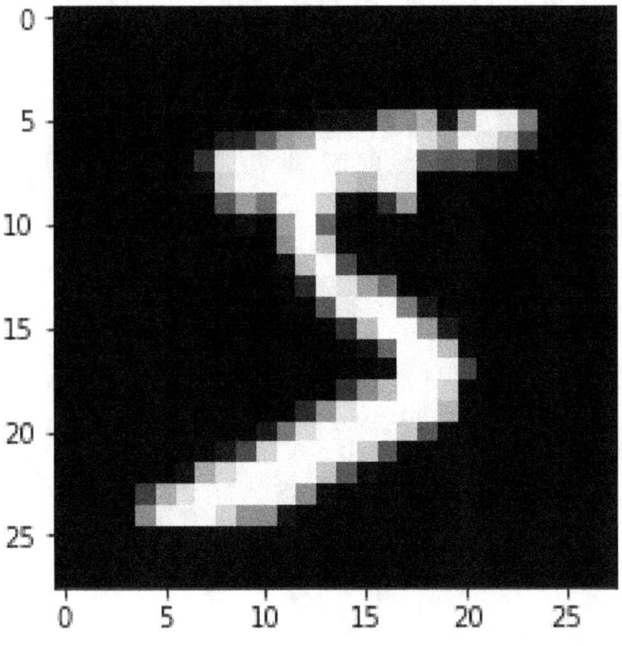

Figure 7.7: mnist sample digits

7.5.2 Dataset transforms

Pytorch allows us to put apply any transform on a dataset, by passing a transform operation to the dataset. If you read the __getitem__ implementation of MNIST dataset carefully, you will find the following code:

```
def __getitem__(self, index):
  # ...
  # ...
  if self.transform is not None:
      img = self.transform(img)

  if self.target_transform is not None:
```

```
        target = self.target_transform(target)

    return img, target
```

That means if dataset is initialized with a transform function, the dataset __getitem__ function will apply that transform to the data item before returning to the caller.

Let's see an example:

```
1  # create a transform
2  >>> transform_f=transforms.Compose([transforms.RandomHorizontalFlip()])
3
4  # pass to the dataset
5  >>> training_ds_trans = datasets.MNIST(data_dir,train=True, download=True,  ↩
       transform=transform_f)
6
7  # get an image
8  >>> img3 = training_ds_trans.__getitem__(0)
9
10 >>> plt.imshow(img3[0])
```

Each time you run the Line 3-4, you may get a different flipped image:

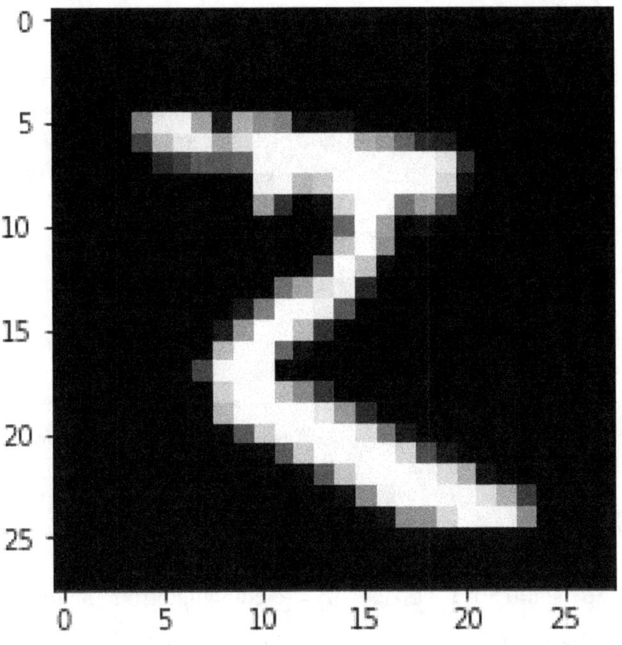

Figure 7.8: mnist transformed sample digits

Actually, you can chain many transforms together, then pass it to dataset together. For example:

```
transform=transforms.Compose([
    transforms.ToTensor(),
    transforms.Normalize((0.1307,), (0.3081,) ])
```

We use transforms.ToTensor to transform the original PIL.Image.Image to pytorch tensor, then we try to normalize it as mean=0.1307 and std=0.3081 on the first dimension. This is called **data normalization**.

Tip

A standard approach is to scale the inputs to have mean 0 and a variance of 1.

It is well-established that networks converge faster if the inputs have been whitened (ie zero mean, unit variances), and are uncorrelated.

Tip

One advanced normalization strategy is called **Batch normalization.**
It allows us to use much higher learning rates, and be less careful about initialization. It also acts as a **regularizer**, in some cases eliminating the need for Dropout. Pytorch provides some very good normalization layers. More details could be found at:
https://pytorch.org/docs/stable/nn.html#normalization-layers

Here is official document about the normalize:

```
Normalize a tensor image with mean and standard deviation.
Given mean: (M1,...,Mn) and std: (S1,..,Sn) for n channels,
this transform will normalize each channel of the input torch.*Tensor
i.e. input[channel] = (input[channel] - mean[channel]) / std[channel]
```

The magic mean=0.1307,std=0.3081 was actually pre-computed from the training set.

There are many pre-defined transforms defined in torchvision package, for example, for images, there are: CenterCrop, Grayscale, RandomCrop, Scale etc.

You can find more transforms at:

https://pytorch.org/docs/stable/torchvision/transforms.html

Pytorch give you the flexibility to define your own transformation as long as you provide a __call__ function. The following is an example of official Resize() implementation.

```
class Resize(object):
    """Resize the input PIL Image to the given size.

    Args:
        size (sequence or int): Desired output size. If size is a sequence like
            (h, w), output size will be matched to this. If size is an int,
            smaller edge of the image will be matched to this number.
            i.e, if height > width, then image will be rescaled to
            (size * height / width, size)
        interpolation (int, optional): Desired interpolation. Default is
```

```
            ``PIL.Image.BILINEAR``
    """

    def __init__(self, size, interpolation=Image.BILINEAR):
        assert isinstance(size, int) or (isinstance(size, Iterable) and len(size) ↩
            == 2)
        self.size = size
        self.interpolation = interpolation

    def __call__(self, img):
        """
        Args:
            img (PIL Image): Image to be scaled.

        Returns:
            PIL Image: Rescaled image.
        """
        return F.resize(img, self.size, self.interpolation)

    def __repr__(self):
        interpolate_str = _pil_interpolation_to_str[self.interpolation]
        return self.__class__.__name__ + '(size={0}, interpolation={1})'.format( ↩
            self.size, interpolate_str)
```

7.5.3 DataLoader

Now we can use torch.utils.data.DataLoader to load the dataset.

The DataLoader is an iterator which provides many features together with dataset:

- a sample (e.g an image) is read from the file on the fly
- transforms are applied on the read sample (e.g.: image) Since one of the transforms could be random, data could be augmented on sampling.
- Batching the data
- Shuffling the data
- Load the data in parallel using multiprocessing workers.

The following showed what parameters DataLoader can take:

```
torch.utils.data.DataLoader(dataset, batch_size=1, shuffle=False,
  sampler=None, batch_sampler=None, num_workers=0,
  collate_fn=<function default_collate>, pin_memory=False, drop_last=False,
  timeout=0, worker_init_fn=None)

Data loader. Combines a dataset and a sampler, and provides
single- or multi-process iterators over the dataset.

Parameters:

dataset (Dataset) - dataset from which to load the data.

batch_size (int, optional) - how many samples per batch to load (default: 1).

shuffle (bool, optional) - set to True to have the data reshuffled at every epoch (default: False).

sampler (Sampler, optional) - defines the strategy to draw samples from the dataset.
If specified, shuffle must be False.

batch_sampler (Sampler, optional) - like sampler, but returns a batch of
indices at a time. Mutually exclusive with batch_size, shuffle, sampler, and drop_last.

num_workers (int, optional) - how many subprocesses to use for data loading.
0 means that the data will be loaded in the main process. (default: 0)

collate_fn (callable, optional) - merges a list of samples to form a mini-batch.

pin_memory (bool, optional) - If True, the data loader will copy tensors
into CUDA pinned memory before returning them.

drop_last (bool, optional) - set to True to drop the last incomplete batch,
if the dataset size is not divisible by the batch size.
If False and the size of dataset is not divisible by the batch size,
then the last batch will be smaller. (default: False)

timeout (numeric, optional) - if positive, the timeout value for collecting
```

```
a batch from workers. Should always be non-negative. (default: 0)

worker_init_fn (callable, optional) - If not None, this will be called on
each worker subprocess with the worker id (an int in [0, num_workers - 1])
as input, after seeding and before data loading. (default: None)
```

Most of the parameters above are easy to understand. One parameter of interest is **collate_fn**. We can specify how exactly the samples need to be batched using collate_fn. However, default collate should work fine for most use cases.

In our MNIST example, Line 90-96, we load the training dataset using:

```
batch_size=args.batch_size, shuffle=True
```

Similarly, in Line 97-102, we load testing dataset.

Let's try to get an image from this dataloader:

```
# our transforms
>>> transform_f2 = transforms.Compose([transforms.ToTensor(),
transforms.Normalize((0.1307,), (0.3081,)) ])

# load the MNIST data with transforms
>>> training_ds_2 = datasets.MNIST(data_dir, train=True, download=True,
transform=transform_f2)

# use DataLoader to load/sample data
>>> train_loader = torch.utils.data.DataLoader(training_ds_2, batch_size=4, ↩
    shuffle=True)

# since it is a python generator, we can get its iterator
>>> dataloader_iterator = iter(train_loader)

# now use iterator, we can get samples
>>> sample1 = next(dataloader_iterator)

# the sample has batchsize=4 image samples with digits: 8,8,5,1
>>> sample1
[tensor([[[[-0.4242, -0.4242, -0.4242,  ..., -0.4242, -0.4242, -0.4242],
          ...,
```

```
          [-0.4242, -0.4242, -0.4242,  ..., -0.4242, -0.4242, -0.4242]]],

        [[[-0.4242, -0.4242, -0.4242,  ..., -0.4242, -0.4242, -0.4242],
          ...,
          [-0.4242, -0.4242, -0.4242,  ..., -0.4242, -0.4242, -0.4242]]],

        [[[-0.4242, -0.4242, -0.4242,  ..., -0.4242, -0.4242, -0.4242],
          ...,
          [-0.4242, -0.4242, -0.4242,  ..., -0.4242, -0.4242, -0.4242]]],

        [[[-0.4242, -0.4242, -0.4242,  ..., -0.4242, -0.4242, -0.4242],
          ...,
          [-0.4242, -0.4242, -0.4242,  ..., -0.4242, -0.4242, -0.4242]]]]),
 tensor([8, 8, 5, 1])]

# get the first image tensor from batched samples, should be 8
>>> sample_img = sample1[0][0]

# transformation operation from tensor to PILImage
>>> tensor_2_img = transforms.ToPILImage()

# transform the sample_img to a real PHIL image
>>> img5 = tensor_2_img(sample_img)
>>> plt.imshow(img5)
```

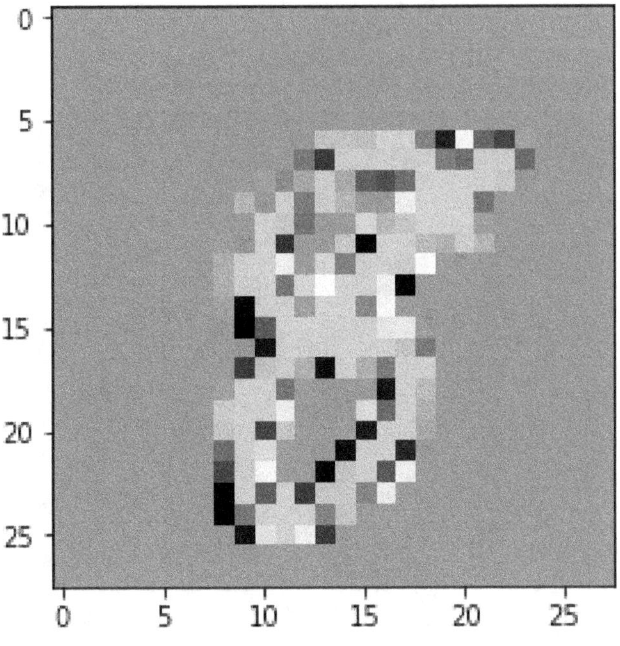

Figure 7.9: an image (8) from dataloader's batched sample

We can verify the last image is 1:

```
# last one from the batch
>>> img6 = tensor_2_img(sample1[0][3])
>>> plt.imshow(img6)
```

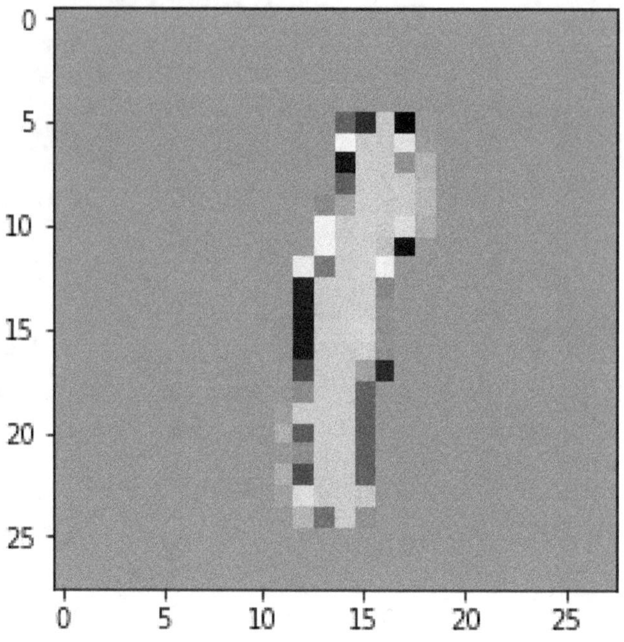

Figure 7.10: another image (1) from dataloader's batched sample

Warning

pytorch only support mini-batches!, According to:
https://seba-1511.github.io/tutorials/beginner/former_torchies/nn_tutorial.html
torch.nn only supports mini-batches. The entire torch.nn package only supports inputs that is a mini-batch of samples and NOT a single sample. For example, nn.Conv2d will take in a 4D Tensor of nSamples x nChannels x Height x Width. If you have a single sample, just use input.unsqueeze(0) to add a fake batch dimension.

7.6 MNIST training and evaluation process

Now we know how the data is loaded, we can look how we train and evaluate the data.

The whole training and evaluation process is similar to what we introduced in the previous chapter. More details as following:

- Line 62-82 parse the parameters.
- Line 83-87 check if there is a GPU or not.
- Line 85 just set the seed for generating random numbers in pytorch using torch.manual_seed.
- Line 90-102 load training and testing dataset. s
- Line 105, we create a DNN instance. The to(device) just put tensors onto the specified device (CPU or GPU).
- Line 106, we create an SGD optimizer. We will talk about different optimizers later.
- Line 108-110, we will run the training/testing for args.epochs times.
- Line 28-40 defines we will train the data. It is a pretty much standard code of training in pytorch just like that in our previous chapter.

One thing that is need to be noted is we put the model into training mode in Line 29 by calling ((train())).

Also in Line 43 while in test function, we put the model into evaluation mode by calling ((eval())).

Pytorch document says:

```
train(mode=True)
Sets the module in training mode.

This has any effect only on certain modules.
See documentations of particular modules for details of their behaviors
in training/evaluation mode, if they are affected, e.g. Dropout, BatchNorm, etc.

eval()
Sets the module in evaluation mode.

This has any effect only on certain modules. See documentations of particular
modules for details of their behaviors in training/evaluation mode,
if they are affected, e.g. Dropout, BatchNorm, etc.
```

For example Dropout works as a regularization for preventing overfitting during training. It randomly zeros the elements of inputs in Dropout layer on forward call. It should be disabled during testing (model.eval()) since we want to use the full model (no element is masked).

- Line 34, we use nll_loss to calculate the loss between our prediction and the ground truth. We will talk about different loss functions shortly.
- Line 42-59 defines how we test/evaluate our model. The code is similar to the training code.

7.7 loss function

In line 34, we use nll_loss to calculate the loss.

what is nll_loss? Why do we want to use this loss function?

Well, **loss function** is the hardcore in any neural network.

It is used to **measure the inconsistency between the predicted value and actual target/label, and can guide an optimizer to adjust the parameters**.

Pytorch documents list several loss functions:

https://pytorch.org/docs/stable/nn.html#loss-functions

If you do not have much deep learning background knowledge, it is difficult to understand those descriptions.

Another natural question for a newcomer is: which loss function to use?

This section will try to fill the gap.

First, we will go over several loss functions, then we will give some guideline on how to choose a loss function.

Please skip some sections if you are familiar with them.

7.7.1 MSELoss, L2 loss

MSELoss is also called **mean squared error (MSE) or mean squared deviation (MSD), or mean squared prediction error**.

It refers to the mean value of the squared deviations of the predictions from the true values.

It is commonly used in a regression problem.

MSELoss is basically:

SUM($(Y_i - Y)^2$) / N,

where Y_i is a target prediction from our model, Y is the real target value, N is total number of samples.

L2 loss is mathematically similar to MSE, the only difference is it does not have a division by N.

One benefit of the square loss function is its simplicity, sometimes we can get an analytic solution if we use this loss function.

But square loss function tends to penalize outliers excessively, leads to slower convergence rates (with regards to sample complexity) than that for the logistic loss or hinge loss functions.

Many loss functions in pytorch can take **reduction** parameter.

For example, a MSELoss is defined as:

```
torch.nn.MSELoss(size_average=None, reduce=None, reduction='mean')

reduction (string, optional) - Specifies the reduction to apply to the output:
'none' | 'mean' | 'sum'.

'none': no reduction will be applied,

'mean': the sum of the output will be divided by the number of elements in the ↩
    output,

'sum': the output will be summed.

Note: size_average and reduce are in the process of being deprecated,
and in the meantime, specifying either of those two args will override reduction.
Default: 'mean'
```

Please note: size_average, reduce are deprecated, we should use reduction.

By default, the reduction is set as "mean", so most of the time we do not need to overwrite it.

7.7.2 L1Loss, Mean Absolute Error

Mean Absolute Error (MAE) is quantity used to measure how close the forecasts or predictions are to the eventual outcomes.

It is basically:

SUM($|Y_i$ -Y|) / N

L1 loss is mathematically similar to MAE, but only does not have the division by n.

MAE is more robust to outliers since it does not make use of the square.

7.7.3 Mean Absolute Percentage Error

Mean Absolute Percentage Error (MAPE) is a variant of MAE.

It is basically defined as:

SUM($|Y_i$-Y)/Y|)/N

where Y_i is a target prediction from our model, and Y is the real target value.

MAPE sounds very simple and convincing, but has major drawbacks:

- It cannot be used if there are zero values as that would mean a division by zero.
- It tends to select a model whose forecasts are too low.

7.7.4 SmoothL1Loss, Huber loss

SmoothL1Loss (also called huber loos) is in the middle of L2Loss and L1Loss.

$$\text{loss}(x, y) = \frac{1}{n} \sum_i z_i$$

where z_i is given by:

$$z_i = \begin{cases} 0.5(x_i - y_i)^2, & \text{if } |x_i - y_i| < 1 \\ |x_i - y_i| - 0.5, & \text{otherwise} \end{cases}$$

Figure 7.11: SmoothL1Loss or Huber loss

It is less sensitive to outliers than the MSELoss and in some cases prevents exploding gradients.

7.7.5 Mean Squared Logarithmic Error

Mean Squared Logarithmic Error (MSLE) is a variant of MSE.

$$\mathcal{L} = \frac{1}{n}\sum_{i=1}^{n}\left(\log(y^{(i)}+1) - \log(\hat{y}^{(i)}+1)\right)^2$$

Figure 7.12: msle definition

It is usually used when we do not want to penalize huge differences in the predicted and the actual values when both predicted and true values are huge numbers.

MSLE penalizes under-estimates more than over-estimates.

Pytorch does not provide this loss by default, but you can easily implement it.

7.7.6 logcosh

Log-cosh is the **logarithm of the hyperbolic cosine**.

$$L(y, y^p) = \sum_{i=1}^{n} \log(\cosh(y_i^p - y_i))$$

Figure 7.13: logcosh function

log(cosh(x)) is approximately equal to (x ** 2) / 2 for small x and to abs(x) - log(2) for large x.

This means that *logcosh* works mostly like the mean squared error, but will not be so strongly affected by the occasional wildly incorrect prediction.

Pytorch does not provide this loss by default, but you can easily implement it.

All the above functions are good for regression loss.

7.7.7 NLLLoss, Negative Log-Likelihood Loss

NLLLoss is useful to train a classification problem with number of C classes.

Negative Log-Likelihood is simply calculated as:

L(y) = - Log(y)

Please be noted: this is summed for all the **correct classes**.

For example, a binary classifier output (0.7, 0.3):

- If the first one matches with ground truth target with probability 0.7, the NLLLoss is:
  -log(0.7) = 0.3567
- If the second one matches the target, then the NLLLoss is:
  -log(0.3) = 1.2039

So in the first case, our classifier predicts the correct result with higher probability, our loss is: 0.35. In the second case, where we predict the correct result with a lower probability, our loss is: 1.2039.

That means we have a higher loss in the second case. It is reasonable as we predict the correct results with lower probability/confidence.

For any other multi-classification classifier, we are summing the loss function to all the correct classes. **Thus whenever the network assigns high confidence at the correct class, the loss is low, but when the network assigns low confidence at the correct class, the loss is high.**

The input to this loss is: (log_softmax, target), where the target that this loss expects is a class index (0 to C-1, where C = number of classes).

That is why LogSoftmax and NLLLoss are often used together.

We can easily obtain log-probabilities in a neural network by adding a LogSoftmax layer in the last layer of our network.

In this MNIST example, we output log_softmax in Line 26, then we calculate loss using NLLLoss in Line 34. The target in Line 34 is a digit index 0-9.

More details could be found at:

https://pytorch.org/docs/stable/nn.html#nllloss

7.7.8 CrossEntropyLoss

Cross entropy measures the divergence between two probability distributions.

It is a quantity from the field of Information Theory that measures the distance between probability distributions (In ML case, it's the distance between a ground-truth distribution and our model's predictions).

If the cross-entropy is large, it means the difference between the two distributions is large. Otherwise, if the cross-entropy is small, it means those two distributions are similar to each other.

Generally, comparing to quadratic cost function, cross-entropy cost function has the advantages of fast convergence and is more likely to reach global optimization.

It is defined as:

$$\mathcal{L} = -\frac{1}{n}\sum_{i=1}^{n}\left[y^{(i)}\log(\hat{y}^{(i)}) + (1-y^{(i)})\log(1-\hat{y}^{(i)})\right]$$

Figure 7.14: cross entropy definition

where y is the probability measured from training/testing dataset, y^ is the probability predicted by the model.

For example, for a NN with softmax as the last output layer with 10 outputs:

(1) we can calculate the probability distribution $y^{(i)}$ (i=0,...,9) using softmax based on ground truth data (labels).

(2) we can also calculate the probability distribution $y^{(i)}$ using softmax from the training dataset, thus we can get the loss.

For more mathematical details, see Wikipedia:

https://en.wikipedia.org/wiki/Cross_entropy

The unique thing in pytorch is:
CrossEntropyLoss combines nn.LogSoftmax() and nn.NLLLoss() in one single class.

The input to this loss is: (some_input_with_C_class, target), where the input is a C-dimensional data, and the target that this loss expects is a class index (0 to C-1, where C = number of classes).

If we want to use CrossEntropyLoss in MNIST example, we can remove Line 26, just return in Line 25, then in Line 34, we just need to use CrossEntropyLoss(output, target).

7.7.9 BCELoss, Binary Cross Entropy

BCELoss or Binary Cross Entropy is similar to Cross-Entropy, except that is normally used in **binary classification**, where the target label is assumed to take values 0 or 1.

It is often used with a sigmoid activation function.

7.7.10 BCEWithLogitsLoss, Binary Cross Entropy + Sigmoid

BCEWithLogitsLoss combines a Sigmoid layer and the BCELoss in one single class.

According to pytorch document:

```
This version is more numerically stable than
using a plain Sigmoid followed by a BCELoss as,
by combining the operations into one layer,
we take advantage of the log-sum-exp trick for numerical stability.
```

That means we should try to use BCEWithLogitsLoss instead of BCELoss, Sigmoid separately especially for binary classification problems.

7.7.11 MultiLabelMarginLoss, MultiLabelSoftMarginLoss, MultiMarginLoss

If one obj need to be classified into multiple classes or multiple labels, we need to those loss functions: MultiLabelMarginLoss, MultiLabelSoftMarginLoss, MultiMarginLoss.

Since many problems do not need multiple labels, I will not spend much time on it, you can read more documents at:

https://pytorch.org/docs/stable/nn.html#multilabelmarginloss

https://pytorch.org/docs/stable/nn.html#multilabelsoftmarginloss

https://pytorch.org/docs/stable/nn.html#multimarginloss

7.7.12 KLDivLoss, kullback leibler divergence

In mathematical statistics, the **Kullback–Leibler divergence** (also called **relative entropy**) is another measure of how one probability distribution diverges from a second expected probability distribution.

On one hand, it is similar to cross_entropy, on the other hand, there are some differences.

Information theory tells us that the **entropy** H(p) (calculated) from of a distribution p is an absolute theoretical lower bound limit (minimum bits) we can achieve, so that we can losslessly compress/encode data from p by using an optimal code designed for p, for example, assigning shorter code words to higher probability data/events.

For two probability distributions p, q, DKL(p//q) can be interpreted as the expected number of extra bits needed to encode sample from true distribution p using code optimized for q rather than p.

The cross-entropy H(p,q) measures the average number of bits needed to encode sample from true distribution p using code optimized for q rather than p.

$$
\begin{aligned}
\mathcal{L} &= \frac{1}{n}\sum_{i=1}^{n} \mathcal{D}_{KL}(y^{(i)} || \hat{y}^{(i)}) \\
&= \frac{1}{n}\sum_{i=1}^{n} \left[y^{(i)} \cdot \log\left(\frac{y^{(i)}}{\hat{y}^{(i)}}\right)\right] \\
&= \underbrace{\frac{1}{n}\sum_{i=1}^{n} \left(y^{(i)} \cdot \log(y^{(i)})\right)}_{entropy} \underbrace{-\frac{1}{n}\sum_{i=1}^{n} \left(y^{(i)} \cdot \log(\hat{y}^{(i)})\right)}_{cross-entropy}
\end{aligned}
$$

Figure 7.15: Kullback Leibler (KL) Divergence definition

In short:

H(p,q) = H(p) + DKL(p//q)

When comparing a distribution q against a fixed reference distribution p, cross-entropy and KL divergence are identical up to an additive constant as p is fixed. In this case, it would be equivalent to say that we're minimizing the KL divergence or minimizing cross-entropy.

But if p is not fixed, cross-entropy and KL divergence are different.

A KL divergence of 0 indicates that we can expect similar, if not the same, the behavior of two different distributions. The bigger a KL divergence value, the bigger that those two distributions will behave differently.

KL divergence is a useful distance measure for continuous distributions, and is often useful when performing direct regression over the space of (discretely sampled) continuous output distributions.

In pytorch, the input given to KLDivloss is expected to contain log-probabilities. However, unlike NLLLoss, the input is not restricted to a 2D Tensor. The targets are given as probabilities (i.e. without taking the logarithm).

Tip

KL Divergence can not be used as a distance metric as is not symmetric.

Interesting readers can read more at:

https://en.wikipedia.org/wiki/Entropy_(information_theory)

https://en.wikipedia.org/wiki/Kullback%E2%80%93Leibler_divergence

https://en.wikipedia.org/wiki/Cross_entropy

https://www.countbayesie.com/blog/2017/5/9/kullback-leibler-divergence-explained

https://isaacchanghau.github.io/post/loss_functions/

7.7.13 CosineEmbeddingLoss, Cosine Proximity

Cosine Proximity, also called **cosine similarity**, is a measure of similarity between two non-zero vectors (in ML world, they refer to predicted vector and actual vector) of an inner product space that measures the cosine of the angle between them.

$$\mathcal{L} = -\frac{\mathbf{y} \cdot \hat{\mathbf{y}}}{||\mathbf{y}||_2 \cdot ||\hat{\mathbf{y}}||_2} = -\frac{\sum_{i=1}^{n} y^{(i)} \cdot \hat{y}^{(i)}}{\sqrt{\sum_{i=1}^{n} \left(y^{(i)}\right)^2} \cdot \sqrt{\sum_{i=1}^{n} \left(\hat{y}^{(i)}\right)^2}}$$

Figure 7.16: cosine_proximity function

The unit vectors are similar if they're parallel and dissimilar if they're orthogonal (perpendicular).

In pytorch, CosineEmbeddingLoss is similar to regular cosine proximity, it is defined as: given input tensors x1,x2 and target/label with values 1 or -1 where 1 means similar, and -1 means dissimilar the loss for each sample is:

$$\text{loss}(x, y) = \begin{cases} 1 - \cos(x_1, x_2), & \text{if } y == 1 \\ \max(0, \cos(x_1, x_2) - \text{margin}), & \text{if } y == -1 \end{cases}$$

Figure 7.17: pytorch CosineEmbeddingLoss

It is typically used for learning nonlinear embeddings or semi-supervised learning.

7.7.14 PoissonNLLLoss

PoissonNLLLoss means negative log-likelihood loss with the Poisson distribution of target.

The Poisson loss function is a measure of how the predicted distribution diverges from the expected distribution, the Poisson as loss function is a variant from Poisson Distribution.

$$\mathcal{L} = \frac{1}{n} \sum_{i=1}^{n} \left(\hat{y}^{(i)} - y^{(i)} \cdot \log(\hat{y}^{(i)})\right)$$

Figure 7.18: poisson loss function

BTW, the choice of a loss function is really a choice about the assumed noise distribution.

For example, a mean-squared error loss function corresponds to an assumption that the noise in the system to be modeled is Gaussian. A Poisson loss function corresponds to an assumption that the noise in the system to be modeled is Poisson.

Please read more at:

```
https://matrixmashing.wordpress.com/2017/01/28/what-is-the-appropriate-loss- ↩
    function-for-modeling-neural-responses/
```

7.7.15 HingeEmbeddingLoss

Hinge loss is a loss function used for training classifiers. It is used for “maximum-margin” classification, most notably for support vector machines (SVMs).

$$\mathcal{L} = \frac{1}{n} \sum_{i=1}^{n} \max(0, 1 - y^{(i)} \cdot \hat{y}^{(i)})$$

Figure 7.19: hinge function

Note $y^{(i)}$ should be the "raw" output of the classifier’s decision function, not the predicted class label.

The hinge loss provides a relatively tight, convex upper bound on the 0–1 indicator function.

One important property of hinge loss is:
data points far away from the decision boundary contribute nothing to the loss, the solution will be the same as those points removed.

Another variant of Hinge loss is called **squared_hinge**,

$$\mathcal{L} = \frac{1}{n} \sum_{i=1}^{n} \left(\max(0, 1 - y^{(i)} \cdot \hat{y}^{(i)}) \right)^2$$

Figure 7.20: squared hinge function

Pytorch's HingeEmbeddingLoss measures the loss given an input tensor x and a label tensor y containing values (1 or -1). This is usually used for measuring whether two inputs are similar or dissimilar, e.g. using the L1 pairwise distance as x, and is typically used for learning nonlinear embeddings or semi-supervised learning.

Please see more details at:

https://en.wikipedia.org/wiki/Hinge_loss

http://yaroslavvb.blogspot.com/2007/06/log-loss-or-hinge-loss.html

https://en.wikipedia.org/wiki/Loss_functions_for_classification

7.7.16 CTCLoss

CTCLoss stands for Connectionist Temporal Classification, it is very useful to handle sequence data.

We will explore this loss function in the chapter of Optical character recognition (OCR).

7.7.17 other loss functions

Some other loss functions in pytorch, such as MarginRankingLoss, SoftMarginLoss, TripletMarginLoss have not been covered in this book, if needed, you can refer to https://pytorch.org/docs/stable/nn.html#loss-functions for more details.

7.7.18 how to choose loss/cost functions

Choosing a good loss function could be a very complicated problem. Here are some tips.

In general, the problem we are trying to solve should determine which loss function we can use.

For example, we can use BCEWithLogitsLoss as its loss function for a binary classification task such as predicting an image being a face or not, as it is a two-class classification problem.

For a many-class classification problem, we usually use softmax as the last output layer with NLLLoss as loss function, or we can use CrossEntropyLoss without a softmax layer.

For a regression problem, we can choose the mean-squared error.

The following figure could help us choose a loss function based on our problem: classification or regression.

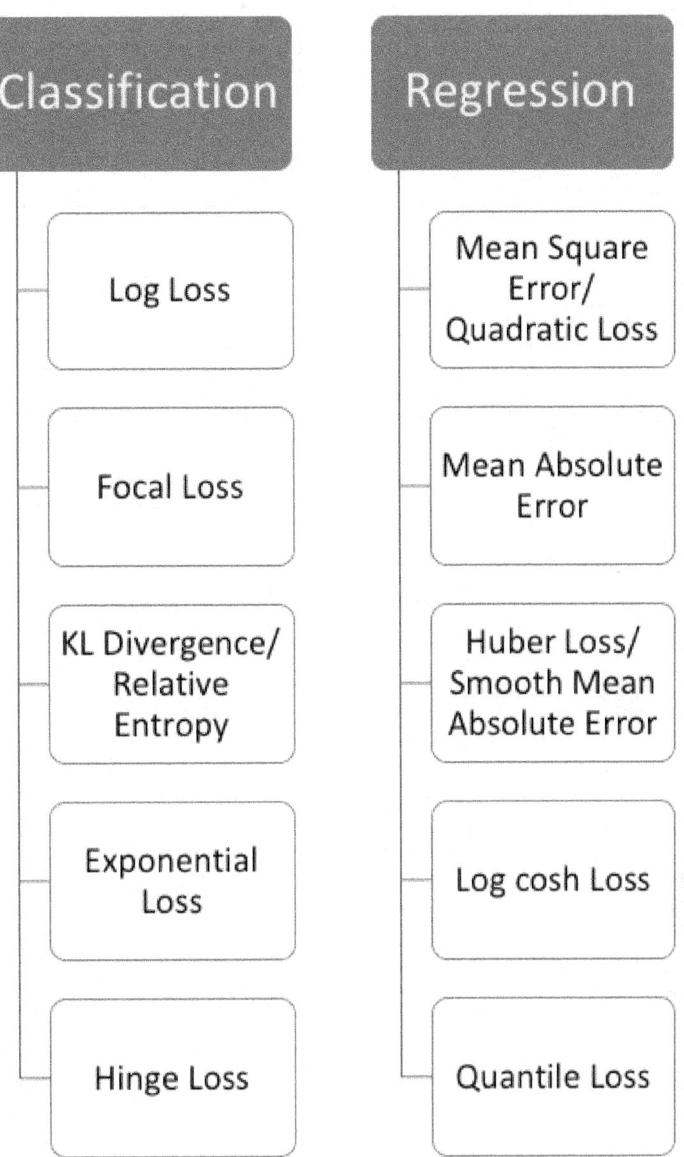

Figure 7.21: loss function regression vs classification

Please note the above method of choosing a loss function is just a rule of thumb, not a strict rule. We should base the problem type to choose the last layer and related loss function.

The following table could help us to choose a loss function. (copied from https://www.dlology.com/blog/how-to-choose-last-layer-activation-and-loss-function/)

Table 7.1: Last-layer activation and loss function combinations

Problem type	Last-layer activation	Loss function	Example
Binary classification	-	BCWWithLogitsLoss	Dog vs cat, Sentiment analysis(pos/neg)
Multi-class, single-label classification	softmax	NLLLoss (or CrossEntropyLoss without softmax)	MNIST has 10 classes single label (one prediction is one digit)
Multi-class, multi-label classification	sigmoid	MultiLabelMarginLoss, MultiLabelSoftMargin-Loss, MultiMarginLoss	News tags classification, one blog can have multiple tags
Regression to arbitrary values	None	mse	Predict house price(an integer/float point)
Regression to values between 0 and 1	sigmoid	mse or BCELoss	Engine health assessment where 0 is broken, 1 is new

Sometimes, there's no good preexisting loss function for our problem, we need to define a customized cost function. Designing an appropriate loss function itself will become essential to solve these kind of problems.

For example, a famous Neural-Style algorithm used a carefully designed loss function to capture both content loss and style loss, thus it allows you to take an image and reproduce it with a new artistic style.

Interesting readers can read an excellent tutorial at:

https://pytorch.org/tutorials/advanced/neural_style_tutorial.html

As you can imagine, to design a suitable customized loss function requires us having a very deep domain knowledge, the good news is pytorch will not limit you, you are powered to write whatever loss function it needs to be.

7.8 optimizer

In line 106, we specify an optimizer SGD. What is it?

The optimizer is a mechanism that machine learning network update its learning parameters based on training data and loss function.

Many popular optimize algorithms used in NN are based on **gradient descent**, which are often used as a black-box optimizer. Please see backpropagation in Chapter 2 for the high-level overview.

Pytorch provides many optimizers, see the document at:

https://pytorch.org/docs/stable/optim.html

So which one should we use?

In this section, I will try to list each algorithm's pros and cons, then I will talk about how to choose an optimizer.

Skip those sections if you are familiar with them.

7.8.1 Standard gradient descent, batch gradient descent

Gradient descent is a first-order iterative optimization algorithm finding the minimum of a function.

To find a local minimum of a function using gradient descent, one takes steps proportional to the negative of the gradient (or approximate gradient) of the function at the current point.

Gradient descent is also known as steepest descent.

The learning rate determines the size of the steps we will take to reach a (local) minimum.

You may find more info at:

https://en.wikipedia.org/wiki/Gradient_descent

Batch gradient descent computes the gradient of the cost function w.r.t. the parameters for the entire training data set.

$$w := w - \eta \nabla Q(w) = w - \eta \sum_{i=1}^{n} \nabla Q_i(w)/n,$$

Figure 7.22: how to update weights using batch gradient descent

Batch gradient descent is guaranteed to converge to the global minimum for convex error surfaces and to a local minimum for non-convex surfaces. Because it needs to calculate the gradients for the whole data set to perform just one update, batch gradient descent can be very slow, and is intractable for data sets that don't fit in memory.

7.8.2 torch.optim.SGD, Stochastic gradient descent (SGD)

Not like the batch gradient descent, **stochastic gradient descent** (SGD), also known as **incremental gradient descent**, in contrast, performs an update using gradient descent at random single data point instead of whole data set (remember the cost/loss function is a function of weights over the whole data set).

$$w := w - \eta \nabla Q_i(w).$$

Figure 7.23: how to update weights using batch SGD

The above figure clearly showed the difference that there is a sum in SGD.

It is therefore usually much faster, and can also be used to learn online.

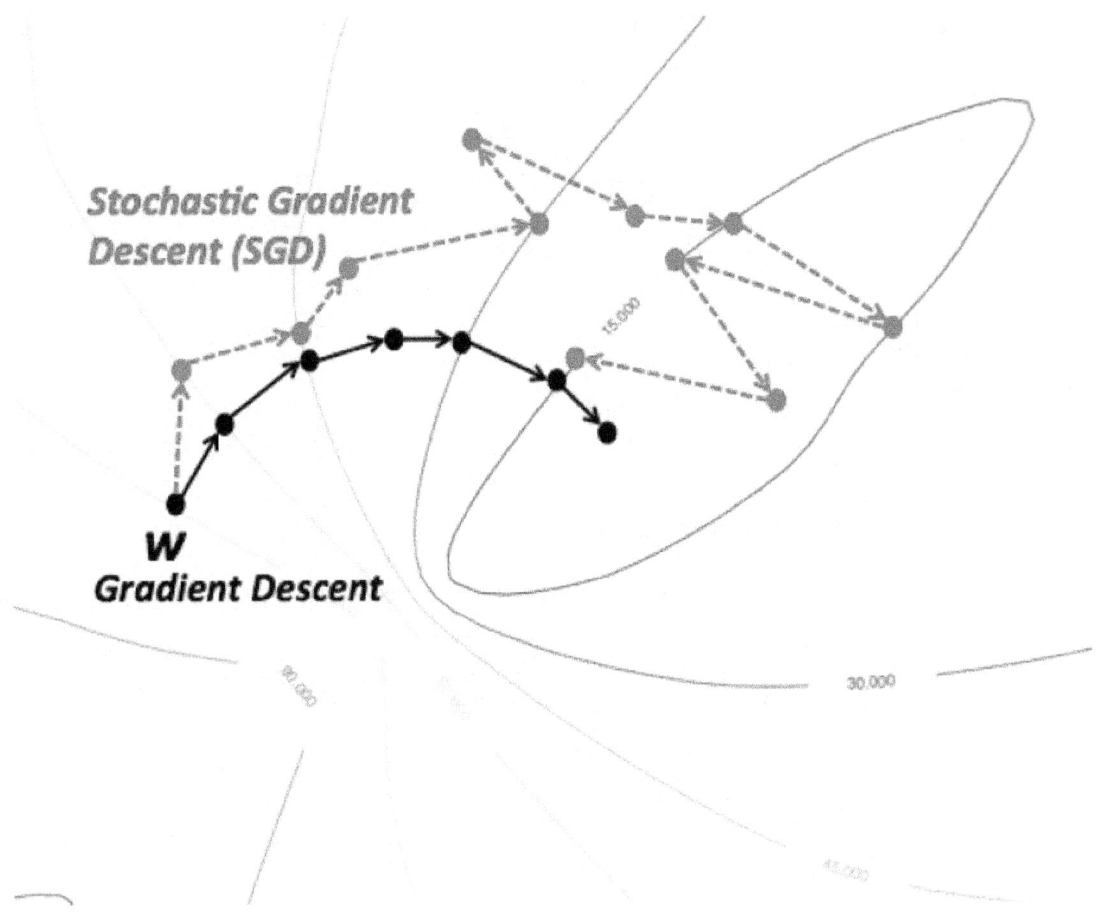

Figure 7.24: standard/batch gradient descent vs SGD.

As shown in the figure above, one con SGD has is: it can perform frequent updates with a high variance that causes the objective function to fluctuate heavily.

In Pytorch, we can call SGD as: torch.optim.SGD(model.parameters(), lr=0.1, momentum=0.9, nesterov=False)

Actually, Pytorch's SGD is an enhanced version, it includes support for momentum, learning rate decay, and Nesterov momentum etc.

Momentum is a method that helps speed up SGD in the relevant direction and preventing oscillations.

$$w := w - \eta \nabla Q_i(w) + \alpha \Delta w$$

Figure 7.25: SGD with momentum

The last term in the figure above is an additional term comparing to normal SGD. That is called momentum, which is the gradient of the weight update.

The momentum increases for dimensions whose gradients point in the same directions and reduces updates for dimensions whose gradients change directions. As a result, we gain faster convergence and reduced oscillation.

7.8.3 Mini-batch gradient descent

Mini-batch gradient descent takes the best of both worlds, and performs an update for every mini-batch of nn training examples.

It is a compromise between computing the true gradient and the gradient at a single example, as it computes the gradient against more than one training example each step.

However, it does not guarantee good convergence.

In pytorch, we can specify the batch size in DataLoader as shown in line 96:

batch_size=args.batch_size

7.8.4 Adaptive gradient descent algorithms

Acute readers probably noticed a problem of previous methods:
we need to specify a learning rate (step size). Setting this parameter too high can cause the algorithm to diverge, setting it too low makes it slow to converge.

Thus, many improvements on the basic stochastic gradient descent algorithm have been proposed and used.

For example, we can make the learning rate a decreasing function η(t) of the iteration number t, such that the first iterations cause large changes in the parameters, while the later ones do only fine-tuning.

Those are called adaptive gradient descent algorithms. Adagrad, Adadelta, RMSprop, Adam are such examples.

7.8.5 torch.optim.Adagrad, AdaGrad

Adaptive gradient (AdaGrad) is a modified stochastic gradient descent with the per-parameter learning rate. It adapts the learning rate to the parameters. Informally, this increases the learning rate for more sparse parameters and decreases the learning rate for less sparse ones.

It is an optimizer with parameter-specific learning rates, which are adapted relative to how frequently a parameter gets updated during training. The more updates a parameter receives, the smaller the updates.

For this reason, it is well-suited for dealing with sparse data. Examples of such applications include natural language processing and image recognition.

Tip

What is **sparse data**, what is **sparse parameters**? Matrices that contain mostly zero values are called sparse, Otherwise called dense.

While designed for convex problems, AdaGrad has been successfully applied to non-convex optimization.

However, its monotonic learning rate usually proves too aggressive and stops learning too early when training deep neural networks.

More details at:
http://en.wikipedia.org/wiki/Stochastic_gradient_descent#AdaGrad

7.8.6 torch.optim.Adadelta, Adadelta

Adadelta is an extension of Adagrad, seeks to reduce its aggressive, monotonically decreasing learning rate.

It is a more robust extension of Adagrad, adapts learning rates based on a moving window of gradient updates, instead of accumulating all past gradients. This way, Adadelta continues learning even when many updates have been done. Compared to Adagrad, in the original version of Adadelta you don't have to set an initial learning rate. In this version, initial learning rate and decay factor can be set.

7.8.7 torch.optim.RMSprop RMSprop

Root Mean Square Propagation (RMSprop) is another method in which the learning rate is adapted for each of the parameters.

It has shown excellent adaptation of learning rates in different applications. RMSProp can be seen as a generalization of Rprop and is capable to work with mini-batches as well as opposed to only full-batches.

RMSprop adjusts the Adagrad method in a very simple way in an attempt to reduce its aggressive, monotonically decreasing learning rate.

The idea is to divide the learning rate for a weight by a running average of the magnitudes of recent gradients for that weight.

RMSprop and Adadelta have both been developed independently around the same time stemming from the need to resolve Adagrad's radically diminishing learning rates.

RMSprop, in fact, is identical to the first update vector of Adadelta, It divides the learning rate by an exponentially decaying average of squared gradients as well.

RMSprop is usually a good choice for recurrent neural networks.

More details at:

https://en.wikipedia.org/wiki/Stochastic_gradient_descent#RMSProp

http://ruder.io/optimizing-gradient-descent/

7.8.8 torch.optim.Adam, Adam

Adaptive Moment Estimation (Adam) is an update to the RMSProp optimizer which is like RMSprop with momentum.

In this optimization algorithm, running averages of both the gradients and the second moments of the gradients are used.

Besides storing an exponentially decaying average of past squared gradients like Adadelta and RMSprop, Adam also keeps an exponentially decaying average of past gradients mtmt, similar to momentum. Whereas momentum can be seen as a ball running down a slope, Adam behaves like a heavy ball with friction, which thus prefers flat minima in the error surface.

AMSGrad is another variant of this Adam, in pytorch you can specify to use it or not by:

amsgrad: boolean.

More details at:

https://en.wikipedia.org/wiki/Stochastic_gradient_descent#Adam

Especially you can read more about AMSGrad at:

http://ruder.io/optimizing-gradient-descent/

7.8.9 torch.optim.Adamax, Adamax

Adamax is a variant of Adam based on the infinity norm.

More details at:

http://ruder.io/optimizing-gradient-descent/

7.8.10 Nadam

Nesterov Adam optimizer (Nadam), Much like Adam is essentially RMSprop with momentum, Nadam is Adam RMSprop with Nesterov momentum.

It is included in torch.optim.SGD. You can pass nesterov=True to torch.optim.SGD.

7.8.11 How to choose an optimizer

In real-world practice, the answer is surprisingly simple. In most cases, it's safe to go with adm/rmsprop and its default learning rate. If the chosen optimizer is not working well, we will try a different optimizer.

Generally speaking, we want to choose an adaptive learning-rate optimizer. The benefit is that we need not tune the learning rate, but likely achieve the best results with the default value.

7.9 summary

After reading this chapter, you should have a solid foundation to understand most online pytorch sample codes with the help from online documents.

In particular, you should know:

- how to use building blocks (conv, pool, dense, fatten layers, etc) from pytorch to write a basic pyotrch DNN module/class.
- how to write a pytorch dataset, dataload to load your raw data.
- how to write pytorch training and evaluation code
- how to choose a loss function generally.
- how to choose an optimizer.

If you have trouble on any of those, I suggest you go back, and read this chapter again.

Chapter 8

Pre-trained model, transfer learning and fine-tuning

Many deep learning projects/models require massive data for training.

One of the most popular benchmark datasets, ImageNet (http://www.image-net.org/), contains one million images from one thousand categories.

According to its website: ImageNet is an image database organized according to the WordNet hierarchy (currently only the nouns), in which each node of the hierarchy is depicted by hundreds and thousands of images. Currently, we have an average of over five hundred images per node.

A very deep network is expensive to train. It usually needs a lot of computing resources to load/train the data (e.g. several weeks of hundreds of machines with GPUs).

Fortunately, many researchers published their training models/results to the public.

For example, Pytorch includes many pre-trained image models: AlexNet, VGG, ResNet, SqueezeNet, DenseNet, Inception v3 etc.

For languages/text, word2vectors and GloVe are two famous pre-trained models.

One natural question is: can we re-use those pre-trained models? And how?

Thankfully, the answer is Yes.

In this chapter, we will show several ways to use pre-trained models.

8.1 Directly use a pre-trained model

Pytorch provides many pre-trained models, see the list here:

https://pytorch.org/docs/stable/torchvision/models.html

We can directly use it, which is the easiest way to re-use a pre-trained model.

Let's look at a simple example to demo how to use a predict function directly from a pre-trained model to do the classification.

Please see the detailed comments inside the code.

```
# pytorch transfer_learning example

import torch
import torchvision.models as models
from torchvision import transforms
from PIL import Image
import torch.nn.functional as F

import numpy as np
import matplotlib.pyplot as plt

# By default, models will be downloaded to your $HOME/.torch folder.
# You can modify this behavior using the $TORCH_MODEL_ZOO variable as follow:
# export TORCH_MODEL_ZOO="/local/pretrainedmodels
# load a pre-trained imagenet model
model = models.resnet18(pretrained=True)
# since we are just evaluate, put the model to eval mode
model.eval()

# load class_names for imagenet
# https://gist.githubusercontent.com/yrevar/942d3a0ac09ec9e5eb3a/raw/238 ↩
    f720ff059c1f82f368259d1ca4ffa5dd8f9f5/imagenet1000_clsidx_to_labels.txt
with open("imagenet1000_clsidx_to_labels.txt") as f:
    class_names = eval(f.read())

# please download this sample file
# for example on linux
# wget https://en.wikipedia.org/wiki/File:African_Bush_Elephant.jpg
img_path = 'elephant.jpg'
```

```

with open(img_path, 'rb') as f:
  with Image.open(f) as img:
    img = img.convert('RGB')

#plt.show()

# according to: https://pytorch.org/docs/stable/torchvision/models.html
# we need to transform before feeding into pretrained model
transform = transforms.Compose([
                               transforms.Resize([224,224]),
                               transforms.ToTensor(),
                               transforms.Normalize(mean=[0.485, 0.456, 0.406],
                                        std=[0.229, 0.224, 0.225])
                               ])

input_tensor = transform(img)          # 3x400x225 -> 3x299x299 size may differ
input_tensor = input_tensor.unsqueeze(0) # 3x299x299 -> 1x3x299x299
input = torch.autograd.Variable(input_tensor, requires_grad=False)

# now do the prediction
output_logits = model(input)

#_, preds = torch.max(output_logits, 1)
top_preds = torch.topk(output_logits, k=3, dim=1)

probs = F.softmax(output_logits, dim=1)[0]

#print( output_logits  )
print( top_preds  )

for pred in top_preds[1][0]:
  real_idx = pred.item()
  print("It is: ", class_names[real_idx], " with prob:", probs[real_idx].item())


# output, we can see the African elephant has the highest score
#(tensor([[19.4503, 18.5631, 15.7322]], grad_fn=<TopkBackward>), tensor([[386, ↩
    101, 385]]))
#It is:  African elephant, Loxodonta africana  with prob: 0.6962595582008362
#It is:  tusker  with prob: 0.28671446442604065
#It is:  Indian elephant, Elephas maximus  with prob: 0.016905518248677254
```

Tip

You can download the complete code of this example from the author's repo (https://github.com/mingewang/pytorch_deep_learning_by_example) at: transfer_learning/pretrained_resnet.py

The code is not difficult to understand at all.

As you can image, even with such a simple script, we can come up with many applications. For example, we can wrap those pre-trained models into a very light library (example: some javascript libs) to do prediction/classification etc.

8.2 transfer learning

In practice, not all applicants can directly use a pre-trained model.

Fortunately, there are other techniques, e.g.: **transfer Learning** and **fine-tuning** etc. to enable us to make use of pre-trained models.

For many practical problems, we typically have access to comparatively small datasets. One example is to train a dog/cat classification model with only hundreds of dog/cat images. In these cases, if we were to train a neural network's weights from scratch, starting from randomly initialized parameters, we would overfit the training set badly.

One approach to get around this problem is to take advantage of a pre-trained model from a large-scale dataset, like ImageNet. We can start with the pre-train weights from a pre-trained model when training on our new, yet much smaller, data set. This process is commonly referred as **transfer-learning/fine-tuning**.

There are several variations of transfer learning.

Sometimes, the initial neural network is only used as a **feature extractor**, which means we freeze every layer prior to the output layer, and simply learn a new output layer.

Another approach is to update all the network's weights for the new task/data, normally we refer it as **fine-tune**. To fine-tune a network, we must first replace the last fully-connected layer with a new one that outputs the desired number of classes. We initialize last layer's weights randomly. Then we continue training as normal. It is common to use a smaller learning rate in this case, purely because of our intuition tells us that we may already be close to a good result.

Some people may differentiate these two terms.

There probably is no clear boundary/definition between transfer learning and fine-tuning, and it seems to have few benefits to differentiate them strictly. Transfer learning may refer to things more broadly, for example, it could include feature extractor and fine-tune, etc.

So in this book, I may use them interchangeably depending on the context, and convenience.

Anyway, either transfer learning or fine-tuning is a machine learning method where a model developed for a task is reused as a starting point for a model on a second task.

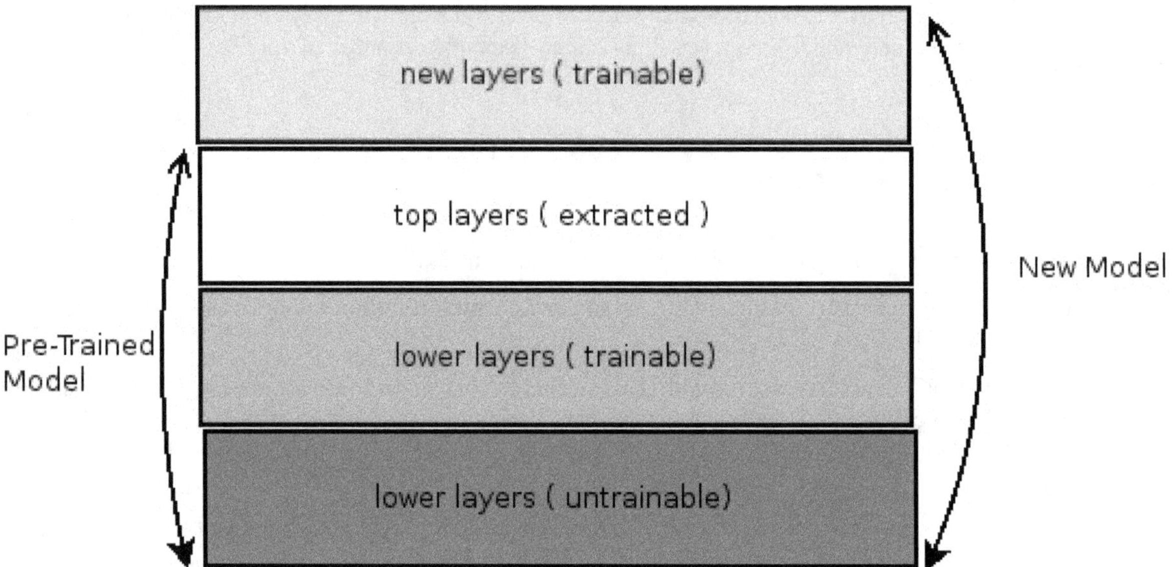

Figure 8.1: transfer learning and fine-tune architecture

Regardless of their difference, the basic idea behind them is:

- we first load a pre-trained model, which includes many layers.
- we can extract/remove some top layers, make some rest layers untrainable, some of them trainable.
- then we add some new layers, thus essentially a new model.
- finally, we train the new model.

Please note how flexible the technique is. It is quite powerful.

In reality, we probably do not have enough data. Thus taking advantage of a pre-trained model can help us solve many problems in hand.

The following table is some rule of thumb on where and how to fine-tune:

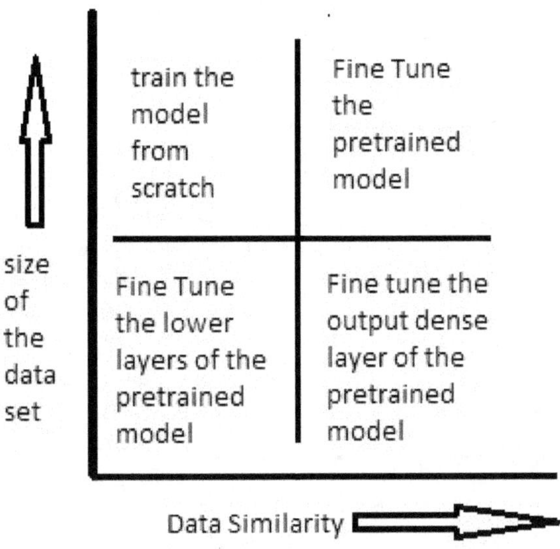

Figure 8.2: transfer learning/fine-tuning

- Right-bottom case: the new dataset is small and similar to the original dataset. Since the data is small, it is not a good idea to fine-tune the ConvNet due to overfitting concerns. Since the data is like the original data, we expect higher-level features in the pre-trained model to be relevant to this dataset as well. Hence, the best idea might be to replace the last layer of a pre-trained model, then train from there.
- Right-upper case: new dataset is large and similar to the original dataset. Since we have more data, we can have more confidence that we won't overfit if we were to try to fine-tune through the full network.
- Left-upper case: the new dataset is large and very different from the original dataset. Since the dataset is very large, we may expect that we can afford to train a model from scratch. However, in practice, it is very often

still beneficial to initialize with weights from a pre-trained model. In this case, we would have enough data and confidence to fine-tune through the entire network.

- Left-bottom case: the new dataset is small but very different from the original dataset. Since the dataset is very different, and data is small, it might not be best to train the model from the top of the network, which contains more dataset-specific features. Instead, it might work better to replace or train a lower/earlier layer.

More details can be found at:

http://cs231n.github.io/transfer-learning/

8.3 bottleneck features extraction

In a special case called **bottleneck features extraction**, we load a pre-trained model with the last fully connected layer removed, then we run the model on our training/validation data, recording the output. That output is called **bottleneck features**. Finally, we train our small model based on the recorded features.

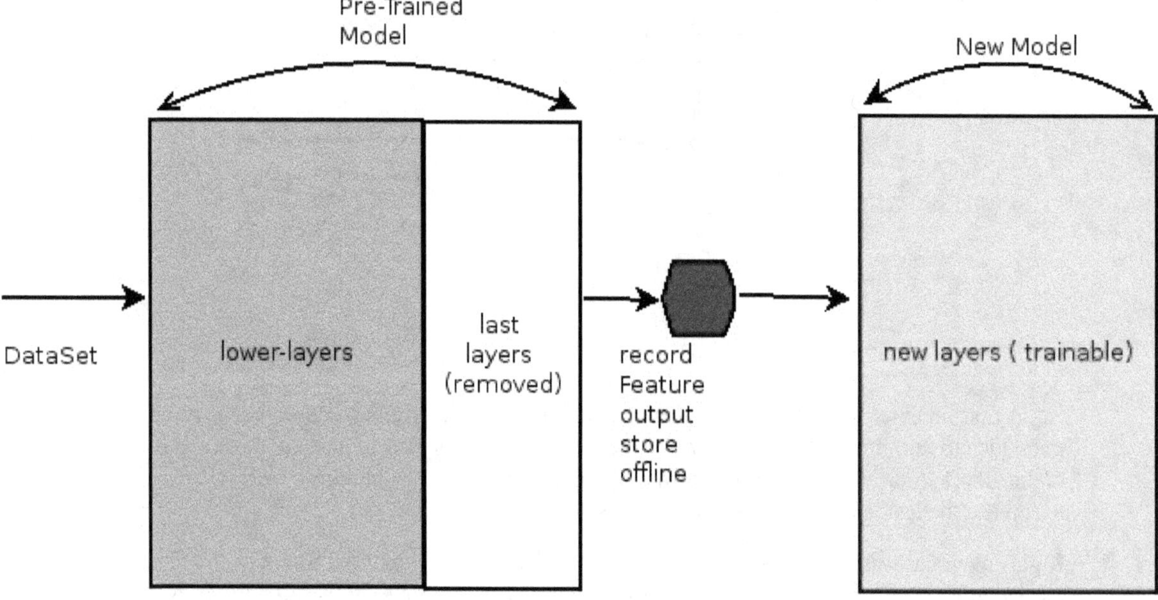

Figure 8.3: bottleneck feature

As shown in the above figure, we stored the features offline instead of adding some news layers on top of the frozen model, the main advantage of this architecture is it can save computing resources. The disadvantage is that the predicted result could be less accurate.

If we do something similar to Figure 8.1, training the whole new model using fine-tune is usually expensive, but it could give us better results.

This bottleneck feature has some other interesting applications, e.g.: image/document clustering, where we do the clustering in the extracted feature space by using bottleneck feature techniques.

Tip

Why can we extract bottleneck features?
The reason is that the features learned from lower layers are likely to be generic.
In CNN, the representations/features learned by the convolutional layers are generic concepts (e.g. edges, textures) over a picture regardless of a particular problem, thus they can be used as features.

Here is an example to show how we freeze all layers in the DNN except for the final layer, then retrain the DNN with the new data. It can be seen as a special fine-tune case.

```
import torch
import torchvision.models as models
from torchvision import transforms
from PIL import Image
import torch.nn.functional as F

model = models.resnet18(pretrained=True)

# freeze the parameters so that the gradients are not computed in backward().
for param in model.parameters():
    param.requires_grad = False

# Parameters of newly constructed modules have requires_grad=True by default
num_ftrs = model.fc.in_features
model.fc = nn.Linear(num_ftrs, 2)

# only parameters of final layer are being optimized
optimizer = optim.SGD(model.fc.parameters(), lr=0.001, momentum=0.9)

# normal pytorch code like get data, training process etc ....
```

The code above showed some important techniques:

- Line 10-11 showed how we can freeze the parameters in a pre-trained model.
- Line 14-15 showed how we can modify a layer in a pre-trained model.
- Line 26 showed how we info optimizer where parameters need to be updated.

The following is another example showing how we can **extract features from an arbitrary intermediate layer**.

```
# feature extractor from any layer example

import torch
import torchvision.models as models
from torchvision import transforms
from PIL import Image
import torch.nn.functional as F

import numpy as np
import matplotlib.pyplot as plt

# extract feature from a layer in this model
# model: pretrained model
# layer_name: layer_name inside that pre-trained model
# output_shape from that layer
# img_path: file path for that image
def extract_feature(model, layer_name, output_shape, img_path):
  with open(img_path, 'rb') as f:
    with Image.open(f) as img:
      img = img.convert('RGB')
      # 1. Load the image with Pillow library
    img = Image.open(img_path)

  # according to: https://pytorch.org/docs/stable/torchvision/models.html
  # we need to transform before feeding into pretrained model
  transform = transforms.Compose([
                                  transforms.Resize([224,224]),
                                  transforms.ToTensor(),
                                  transforms.Normalize(mean=[0.485, 0.456, 0.406],
                                           std=[0.229, 0.224, 0.225])
                                  ])
```

```
    input_tensor = transform(img)          # 3x400x225 -> 3x244x244 size may differ
    input_tensor = input_tensor.unsqueeze(0) # 3x244x244 -> 1x3x244x244
    # Create a PyTorch Variable with the transformed image
    t_input = torch.autograd.Variable(input_tensor, requires_grad=False)

    # 3. Create a vector of zeros that will hold our feature vector
    #    The 'avgpool' layer has an output size of 512
    my_embedding = torch.zeros(output_shape)
    # 4. Define a function that will copy the output of a layer
    def copy_data(m, i, o):
        print (o.data.shape)
        my_embedding.copy_(o.data)

    # Use the model object to select the desired layer
    layer = model._modules.get(layer_name)
    # 5. Attach that function to our selected layer
    h = layer.register_forward_hook(copy_data)
    # 6. Run the model on our transformed image
    model(t_input)
    # 7. Detach our copy function from the layer
    h.remove()
    # 8. Return the feature vector
    return my_embedding

# By default, models will be downloaded to your $HOME/.torch folder.
# You can modify this behavior using the $TORCH_MODEL_ZOO variable as follow:
# export TORCH_MODEL_ZOO="/local/pretrainedmodels
# load a pre-trained imagenet model
model = models.resnet18(pretrained=True)

# we need to watch the output of the model carefully
# then we can choose/decide which feature/layer we want
# in this case, we use: avgpool
# the avgpool is just one layer output from print(model)
# that we want to extract a feature from.
# that is an arbitrary layer for the purpose of this demo.
# feel free to try any other layer
# Need to pay special attention to the shape of this layer
print( model )

# Set model to evaluation mode
```

```
74 model.eval()
75
76 # please download this sample file
77 # for example on linux
78 # wget https://en.wikipedia.org/wiki/File:African_Bush_Elephant.jpg
79 img_path = 'elephant.jpg'
80
81 avg_layer = "avgpool"
82 # observered from its previous layer called layer4[1].bn2
83 # BatchNorm2d(512, eps=1e-05, momentum=0.1, affine=True, track_running_stats=True )
84 output_shape = [1, 512, 1, 1]
85
86 # Now extract feature
87 img_feature = extract_feature(model, avg_layer, output_shape, img_path)
88
89 print( img_feature )
90
91 # now you can do whatever on those features
```

Tip

You can download the complete code of this example from the author's repo (https://github.com/mingewang/pytorch_deep_learning_by_example) at: transfer_learning/feature_extractor.py

It demonstrated several useful techniques:

- Line 47, model._modules.get(layer_name) showed how we can get a specific layer.
- Line 49 layer.register_forward_hook(copy_data) showed how we can install a hook into a model's layer so that we can get pre-process data.

After we get the feature data, we can do anything we want. For example, we can extract features, save to offline, then reload them into a new small model, finally, train the model with the new set of data.

Let's run the above example:

```
sources/transfer_learning$ python feature_extractor.py
ResNet(
  (conv1): Conv2d(3, 64, kernel_size=(7, 7), stride=(2, 2), padding=(3, 3), bias=False)
  (bn1): BatchNorm2d(64, eps=1e-05, momentum=0.1, affine=True, track_running_stats=True)
  (relu): ReLU(inplace)
  (maxpool): MaxPool2d(kernel_size=3, stride=2, padding=1, dilation=1, ceil_mode=False)
  (layer1): Sequential(
    (0): BasicBlock(
      (conv1): Conv2d(64, 64, kernel_size=(3, 3), stride=(1, 1), padding=(1, 1), bias=False)
      (bn1): BatchNorm2d(64, eps=1e-05, momentum=0.1, affine=True, track_running_stats=True)
      (relu): ReLU(inplace)
      (conv2): Conv2d(64, 64, kernel_size=(3, 3), stride=(1, 1), padding=(1, 1), bias=False)
      (bn2): BatchNorm2d(64, eps=1e-05, momentum=0.1, affine=True, track_running_stats=True)
    )
    (1): BasicBlock(
      (conv1): Conv2d(64, 64, kernel_size=(3, 3), stride=(1, 1), padding=(1, 1), bias=False)
      (bn1): BatchNorm2d(64, eps=1e-05, momentum=0.1, affine=True, track_running_stats=True)
      (relu): ReLU(inplace)
      (conv2): Conv2d(64, 64, kernel_size=(3, 3), stride=(1, 1), padding=(1, 1), bias=False)
      (bn2): BatchNorm2d(64, eps=1e-05, momentum=0.1, affine=True, track_running_stats=True)
    )
  )
  (layer2): Sequential(
    (0): BasicBlock(
      (conv1): Conv2d(64, 128, kernel_size=(3, 3), stride=(2, 2), padding=(1, 1), bias=False)
      (bn1): BatchNorm2d(128, eps=1e-05, momentum=0.1, affine=True, track_running_stats=True)
      (relu): ReLU(inplace)
      (conv2): Conv2d(128, 128, kernel_size=(3, 3), stride=(1, 1), padding=(1, 1)
```

```
        , bias=False)
      (bn2): BatchNorm2d(128, eps=1e-05, momentum=0.1, affine=True, track_running_stats=True)
      (downsample): Sequential(
        (0): Conv2d(64, 128, kernel_size=(1, 1), stride=(2, 2), bias=False)
        (1): BatchNorm2d(128, eps=1e-05, momentum=0.1, affine=True, track_running_stats=True)
      )
    )
    (1): BasicBlock(
      (conv1): Conv2d(128, 128, kernel_size=(3, 3), stride=(1, 1), padding=(1, 1), bias=False)
      (bn1): BatchNorm2d(128, eps=1e-05, momentum=0.1, affine=True, track_running_stats=True)
      (relu): ReLU(inplace)
      (conv2): Conv2d(128, 128, kernel_size=(3, 3), stride=(1, 1), padding=(1, 1), bias=False)
      (bn2): BatchNorm2d(128, eps=1e-05, momentum=0.1, affine=True, track_running_stats=True)
    )
  )
  (layer3): Sequential(
    (0): BasicBlock(
      (conv1): Conv2d(128, 256, kernel_size=(3, 3), stride=(2, 2), padding=(1, 1), bias=False)
      (bn1): BatchNorm2d(256, eps=1e-05, momentum=0.1, affine=True, track_running_stats=True)
      (relu): ReLU(inplace)
      (conv2): Conv2d(256, 256, kernel_size=(3, 3), stride=(1, 1), padding=(1, 1), bias=False)
      (bn2): BatchNorm2d(256, eps=1e-05, momentum=0.1, affine=True, track_running_stats=True)
      (downsample): Sequential(
        (0): Conv2d(128, 256, kernel_size=(1, 1), stride=(2, 2), bias=False)
        (1): BatchNorm2d(256, eps=1e-05, momentum=0.1, affine=True, track_running_stats=True)
      )
    )
    (1): BasicBlock(
      (conv1): Conv2d(256, 256, kernel_size=(3, 3), stride=(1, 1), padding=(1, 1), bias=False)
      (bn1): BatchNorm2d(256, eps=1e-05, momentum=0.1, affine=True,
```

```
          track_running_stats=True)
        (relu): ReLU(inplace)
        (conv2): Conv2d(256, 256, kernel_size=(3, 3), stride=(1, 1), padding=(1, 1) ↩
          , bias=False)
        (bn2): BatchNorm2d(256, eps=1e-05, momentum=0.1, affine=True,  ↩
          track_running_stats=True)
      )
    )
    (layer4): Sequential(
      (0): BasicBlock(
        (conv1): Conv2d(256, 512, kernel_size=(3, 3), stride=(2, 2), padding=(1, 1) ↩
          , bias=False)
        (bn1): BatchNorm2d(512, eps=1e-05, momentum=0.1, affine=True,  ↩
          track_running_stats=True)
        (relu): ReLU(inplace)
        (conv2): Conv2d(512, 512, kernel_size=(3, 3), stride=(1, 1), padding=(1, 1) ↩
          , bias=False)
        (bn2): BatchNorm2d(512, eps=1e-05, momentum=0.1, affine=True,  ↩
          track_running_stats=True)
        (downsample): Sequential(
          (0): Conv2d(256, 512, kernel_size=(1, 1), stride=(2, 2), bias=False)
          (1): BatchNorm2d(512, eps=1e-05, momentum=0.1, affine=True,  ↩
            track_running_stats=True)
        )

      (1): BasicBlock(
        (conv1): Conv2d(512, 512, kernel_size=(3, 3), stride=(1, 1), padding=(1, 1) ↩
          , bias=False)
        (bn1): BatchNorm2d(512, eps=1e-05, momentum=0.1, affine=True,  ↩
          track_running_stats=True)
        (relu): ReLU(inplace)
        (conv2): Conv2d(512, 512, kernel_size=(3, 3), stride=(1, 1), padding=(1, 1) ↩
          , bias=False)
        (bn2): BatchNorm2d(512, eps=1e-05, momentum=0.1, affine=True,  ↩
          track_running_stats=True)
      )
    )
    (avgpool): AvgPool2d(kernel_size=7, stride=1, padding=0)
    (fc): Linear(in_features=512, out_features=1000, bias=True)
)
torch.Size([1, 512, 1, 1])
tensor([[[[7.3921e-01]],
```

```
        [[4.9047e-01]],
...
       [[5.6697e-01]]]])
```

8.4 fine-tune

Fine-tune need more involvement. Normally, it means two-pass training.

- For the first pass:
  We first add some layers on top of a pre-trained model. Then we make the pre-trained model layer untrainable, train the new model.
- For the second pass:
  We unfreeze some layers in the pre-trained model, then re-train it again.

Tip

Broadly speaking, the previous feature extraction could be viewed as one type of fine-tuning.

The following is a skeleton of fine-tune example:

```
# pytorch fine tune example
import torch
import torchvision.models as models
from torchvision import transforms
import torch.nn as nn
import torch.optim as optim
from PIL import Image
import torch.nn.functional as F

model = models.resnet18(pretrained=True)

# freeze the parameters so that the gradients are not computed in backward().
for param in model.parameters():
    param.requires_grad = False

```

```
# model last layer
num_ftrs = model.fc.in_features
model.fc = nn.Linear(num_ftrs, 2)

# we can add more layers here by using add_module
# for example: ("my_conv", Conv2d(3, 16, 5, padding=2))
model.add_module("my_fc_2",nn.Linear(2,1))

# only parameters of the two layers are being optimized
# we concatenate those two parameter lists
params = list(model.fc.parameters()) + list(model.my_fc_2.parameters())
optimizer = optim.SGD( params, lr=0.001, momentum=0.9)

print( params )

# normal pytorch code like get data, training process, etc ....
# skip here

##############################################################################
# second pass
# unfreeze the parameters
for param in model.parameters():
    param.requires_grad = True

# for debug/demo you can turn it on
# params is a generator
params = model.parameters()
# turn it to be a list
lst = list(params)
print(lst)
# all parameters are being optimized
optimizer_all = optim.SGD(lst, lr=0.001, momentum=0.9)

# or just pass model.parameters() to it
#optimizer_all = optim.SGD(model.parameters(), lr=0.001, momentum=0.9)

# normal pytorch code like get data, training process, etc ....
# skip here
```

Tip

You can download the complete code of this example from the author's repo (https://github.com/mingewang/pytorch_deep_learning_by_example) at: transfer_learning/fine_tune.py

---

The code should be easy to understand.

- Line 13-14 showed how we can freeze the parameters in a pre-trained model.
- Line 17-18 showed how we can modify a layer in a pre-trained model.
- Line 22 showed how we can add some layers to a pre-trained model.
- Line 26 showed how we info optimizer where parameters need to be updated.
- Line 37-38 showed how we can unfreeze the parameters in a model.

If you run the code, you can see those parameters:

```
sources/transfer_learning$ python fine_tune.py
[Parameter containing:
tensor([[ 0.0295, -0.0374, -0.0184,  ...,  0.0440, -0.0059, -0.0089],
        [-0.0362,  0.0204,  0.0089,  ..., -0.0123, -0.0437,  0.0293]],
       requires_grad=True), Parameter containing:
tensor([0.0012, 0.0157], requires_grad=True), Parameter containing:
tensor([[-0.2101, -0.0983]], requires_grad=True), Parameter containing:
tensor([0.4547], requires_grad=True)]
[Parameter containing:
tensor([[[[-1.0419e-02, -6.1356e-03, -1.8098e-03,  ...,  5.6615e-02,
            1.7083e-02, -1.2694e-02],
          [ 1.1083e-02,  9.5276e-03, -1.0993e-01,  ..., -2.7124e-01,
           -1.2907e-01,  3.7424e-03],
          [-6.9434e-03,  5.9089e-02,  2.9548e-01,  ...,  5.1972e-01,
            2.5632e-01,  6.3573e-02],
          ...,
            3.6887e-01,  1.2455e-01],
          ...,
        0.3472, 0.2890, 0.4740, 0.2230, 0.3630, 0.4015, 0.2446, 0.1897, 0.1460,
        0.1874, 0.2734, 0.2366, 0.3001, 0.2359, 0.2688, 0.3256, 0.2749, 0.2848,
```

```
        0.2299, 0.3001, 0.4818, 0.3074, 0.3164, 0.3114, 0.3549, 0.2859],
       requires_grad=True), Parameter containing:
tensor([[ 0.0295, -0.0374, -0.0184, ..,  0.0440, -0.0059, -0.0089],
        [-0.0362,  0.0204,  0.0089, .., -0.0123, -0.0437,  0.0293]],
       requires_grad=True), Parameter containing:
tensor([0.0012, 0.0157], requires_grad=True), Parameter containing:
tensor([[-0.2101, -0.0983]], requires_grad=True), Parameter containing:
tensor([0.4547], requires_grad=True)]
...
```

8.5 summary

This chapter showed several important techniques to take advantage of pre-trained models. In particular, we learned:

- how to directly use a pre-trained model
- general rule of thumb where to apply transfer learning/fine-tune
- how to do bottleneck feature extraction
- how to fine-tune a pre-trained model

Chapter 9

Recurrent neural network - how to handle sequences data

Recurrent Neural Network (RNN)) is a very useful building block in DNN. It was designed to work with sequence prediction problems, which involve using historical sequence (temporal) information to predict the next value or values in the sequence.

Recall a classical NN layer, e.g. MLP layer (Multilayer Perceptrons layer) has no internal state (memory). That means: in any instance of a single operation (like classifying a single image), the feed-forward network has no information about what it did before. It always starts from whatever state it was trained beforehand. No evolution at all after initial training.

On the contrary, an RNN uses its internal state (memory) to process sequences of inputs. It receives not only a payload (e.g.: image as input), but also its own output from the previous step (and transitively from all previous steps). This way, by training, they can keep some relevant information from the past to the future, thus forming a sort of memory, which will help us to handle tasks such as unsegmented, connected handwriting recognition, speech recognition, language translation, image captioning, etc.

In this chapter, we will learn this important technique with great details.

9.1 Why and where to use RNN

In the previous overview section, we introduced some background information on why we need to use RNN.

Let's go deeper.

9.1.1 finite impulse recurrent network

RNN could indiscriminately refer to two broad classes of networks with a similar general structure, one is called **finite impulse**, the other one is called **infinite impulse**.

According to Wikipedia:

https://en.wikipedia.org/wiki/Recurrent_neural_network

A **finite impulse recurrent network** is a directed acyclic graph that can be unrolled and replaced with a strictly feed-forward neural network, while an **infinite impulse recurrent network** is a directed cyclic graph that can not be unrolled.

For a finite impulse recurrent network case, instead of unrolling to a feedforward neural network, we still prefer to use RNN as it gives us a **better compact computing efficiency, and a natural intuitive way to handle sequence-related problems**.

For example, let's say, we want to output yes/no based on even number of 1 from a sequence of input.

Using feedforward NN, we need to wait for the whole block until end of input, in order to be able to feed the input into the network.

E.g.: 1010101010 -→ Yes for even 1

Let's say, our NN has been trained to predict with input of 8 characters long, to predict an input 11, we need to pad 11 into 1100000000 first, then feed 1100000000 into our network.

If we use a RNN, it works like:

- we feed the first 1 to our RNN, the RNN will output no
- then we feed another input 0, the RNN will output no
- next time we feed new input 1, the RNN will output yes
- . . . , so on

As you can see, using RNN here is very natural, powerful.

Additionally, **a RNN normally requires much fewer parameters comparing to an un-rolled feedforward neural network**.

9.1.2 infinite impulse recurrent network

In the previous example, what if we have infinite input?

We can not use a normal feed-forward NN to train and predict our data, we have to use **infinite impulse recurrent network**.

Tip

RNN is Turing completeness.

Regular feed-forward neural networks are not Turing complete. They are equivalent to a single complicated mathematical function that may do quite a lot of calculations, but doesn't have any ability to perform looping or other control flow operations.

However, this paper:

http://binds.cs.umass.edu/papers/1992_Siegelmann_COLT.pdf

proved the following facts: for any computable function, there exists a finite recurrent neural network (RNN) that can compute it. Furthermore, there exist finite RNNs that are Turing complete, and can, therefore, implement any algorithm.

More detailed discussion at:

https://stats.stackexchange.com/questions/220907/meaning-and-proof-of-rnn-can-approximate-any-algorithm

https://arxiv.org/pdf/1904.05061.pdf

Tip

Turing completeness vs Universal approximation

Quote from: https://cs.stackexchange.com/questions/68820

/confused-between-turing-completeness-and-universal-approximation-are-they-rela

To qualify for "universal approximation", it's enough to be able to approximate all functions of nn variables (for each function, there exists a neural network that approximates it), so it talks about functions on inputs of bounded length.

Turing-completeness requires the ability to compute all computable functions, which is a set of functions that has no fixed upper limit on the number of variables, i.e., it is a set of functions on inputs of unbounded length.

Universal approximation could thus, in some sense, be considered "weaker" than Turing-completeness (though strictly speaking they are incomparable; neither implies the other).

9.1.3 where to use RNN

In a real-world practice, some limitations of the previous non-RNN neural networks (e.g. MLP, CNN) are:

- They normally just accept a fixed-sized vector as input.
  For example, a CNN need a fixed known width/height of the image as input, if not, we have to do some pre-processing such as padding to make the input has the predefined width/height.
- At the same time, they produce only a fixed-sized vector as output (e.g. Probabilities set of different classes).
- When these models perform a prediction, they uses a fixed amount of computational steps (e.g. The number of layers in the model), which will limit its capability to predict.

Anyway, not all problems, especially sequence data problems, can be converted into one with a fixed length inputs and outputs, in those cases, we can try to apply RNN to those problems:

- The problems such as speech recognition/language translation or many other time-series sequence problems, which normally require some context information. It is more intuitive and natural to use a RNN.
- The problem that is hard/impossible to choose a fixed context window, e.g. Infinite input.

Next section will show more applications where RNN shines.

9.1.4 RNN applications

Around 2007, Long short-term memory (LSTM), a type of RNN, started to revolutionize speech recognition.

In 2009, a Connectionist Temporal Classification (CTC) trained LSTM network won pattern recognition contests.

LSTM broke records for improved machine translation, language modeling and multilingual language processing, text-to-speech synthesis, which resulted in the rise of Siri, Cortana, Google voice assistant, Alexa etc.

Combined with convolutional neural networks (CNNs), LSTM also improved automatic image captioning, text into images, and captioning video etc.

RNN can be applied in many areas, to name a few:

- Robot control
- Time series prediction
- Speech recognition
- Rhythm learning
- Music composition

- Grammar learning
- Handwriting recognition
- Human action recognition
- Protein Homology Detection
- Predicting subcellular localization of proteins
- Several prediction tasks in business process management
- Prediction in medical care pathways
- Time series anomaly detection
- Semantic Parsing

The core reason that RNNs are more exciting is that they allow us to operate over sequences of vectors: sequences in the input, the output, or in the most general case both.

Generally, RNN applications can be classified into one-to-one, one-to-many, many-to-one, many-to-many etc as shown in the following diagram:

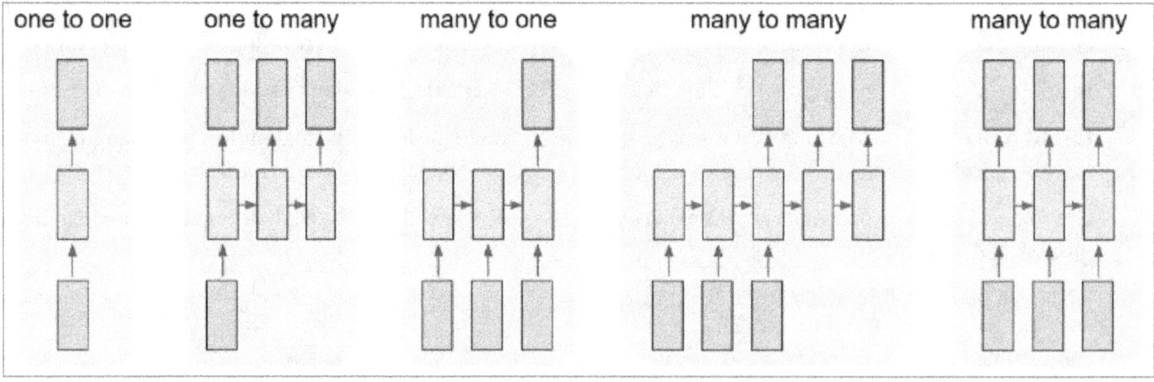

Figure 9.1: RNN applications classification

In the above figure, a rectangle represents a vector/tensor, an arrow represents a function (e.g. matrix multiply etc). Red is input vectors, blue are output vectors, while green represents RNNs.

From left to right, those are applications:

- Applications with fixed-sized input to fixed-sized output.
  In this case RNN is not needed. For example, image classification.
- Applications with a sequence output.
  For example: image captioning which takes an image and outputs a sentence of words.
- Applications with sequence input.
  For example: sentiment analysis where a given sentence is classified as expressing positive or negative sentiment.
- Applications with sequence input and sequence output.
  For example, language translation which reads a sentence in English as input and then outputs a sentence in French.
- Applications with synced sequence input and output.
  For example, video classification where we wish to label each frame of the video.

In all RNN applications above, there is **NO pre-specified constraint on the length of an input sequence**, that is one of the big advantages of an RNN, which is impossible to be handled in a regular feed-forward MLP/CNN.

9.2 RNN basic concept

Get Excited on RNN? Let's look at more technique details!

In a traditional neural network, we assume that all inputs (and outputs) are independent of each other.

But for many tasks, that's not good. If we want to predict the next word in a sentence, we better know which words came before it.

The main idea behind RNN is to make use of sequential information. How?
A loop inside RNN allows such information to persist. The following diagram showed a typical RNN:

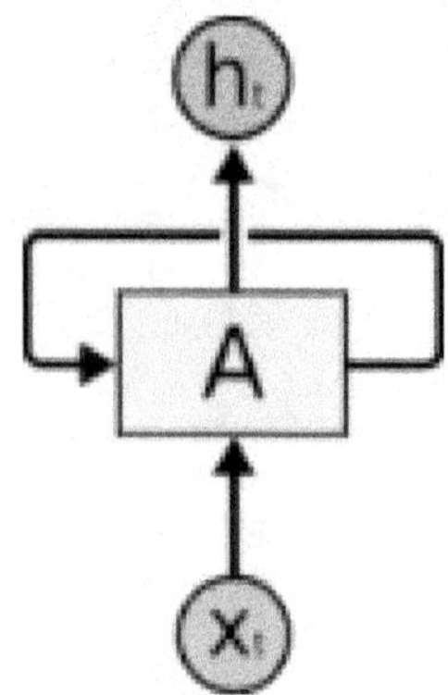
ht
A
Xt
Recurrent Neural Networks have loops.

Figure 9.2: RNN with loop

In the above diagram, a chunk of neural network A, takes an input x_t and outputs a value h_t. A loop allows information to be passed from the previous step of the network to the next.

Tip

More precisely, RNN normally combines the input vector, its state vector and a fixed (but learned) function to produce a new state vector.

The following pseudo-code showed how RNN works:

```
y1 = rnn1.step(x0)
y2 = rnn2.step(y1)
...
y = rnn2.step(yn)
```

In other words, we have many unrolled neural networks: the first NN receives the input vectors, the second NN receives the output of the first NN as its input . . . and so on.

As said before, a finite impulse recurrent neural network can be thought of as multiple copies of the same network, each passing a message to a successor, as shown in the following figure:

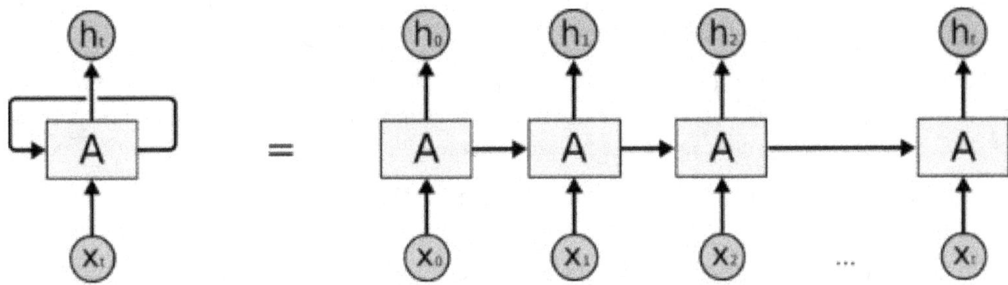

An unrolled recurrent neural network.

Figure 9.3: RNN is an unrolled NN

The chain-like nature architecture reveals that recurrent neural networks are intimately related to sequences and lists, therefore, are the natural architecture for such data. That is all the magic RNN has!

A RNN is called recurrent because it performs the same task for every element of a sequence, with the output depending on the previous computations.

Another way to think about a RNN is that it has a "memory", which captures information about what has been calculated so far.

In theory, RNNs can make use of information in arbitrarily long sequences, but in practice, they are limited to looking back only a few steps (more on this later).

9.3 Pytorch vanilla RNN

Let's look at an example.

For a text input: "hello", we want an RNN model to be able to do this:
The first time RNN see a character “l” input, it can output the target: “l”,
but the second time, it should output the target “o” instead of "l".

So a RNN can not just rely on the input alone, instead, it must use its recurrent connection to keep track of the context to achieve this task.

In pytorch, this type of RNN can be implemented using plain/vanilla RNN such as: torch.nn.RNN, which is good for simple problems that just needs to examine very recent information.

Another example, if we want to predict the last character in “How are you”, it’s quite obvious the next character will be "u", In such cases, the gap between the relevant information and the place that it’s needed is quite small, torch.nn.RNN can learn it easily using the past information.

However, in some cases, it is totally possible that the gap between a prediction position and the position that relevant information resides is very large.

Though, in theory, vanilla RNN is absolutely capable of handling such as “long-term dependencies”, in practice, vanilla RNN cannot learn such long-distance relationships due to the famous vanishing gradient limitation.

Fortunately, Long Short Term Memory networks (LSTM) was invented to rescue.

9.4 Long Short-Term Memory networks (LSTM)

LSTM, as its name suggested, is explicitly designed to avoid the long-term dependency problem.

It was introduced by Hochreiter & Schmidhuber in 1997, and was refined and popularized by many people in the following work.

LSTM works tremendously well on a large variety of problems, and is now widely used.

There are several different architectures of LSTM units. A common architecture is composed of a memory cell, an input gate, an output gate and a forget gate, as shown in the following figure.

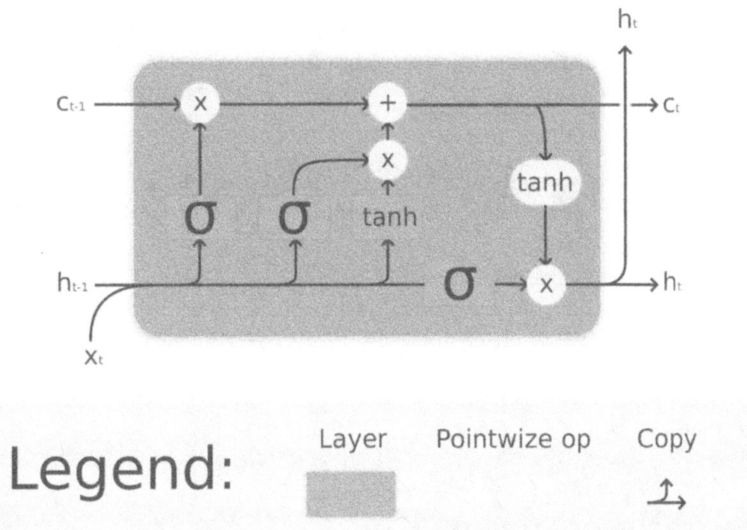

Figure 9.4: LSTM cell architecture

The top line is: C(t-1), C(t), where each c(t) is called **cell state**.

The leftmost gate is called **forget gate**: based on h(t-1), X(t), the gate could output 0 or 1. If 1, let C(t-1) pass; otherwise if 0, no pass at all. **That actually make a long term dependency possible as a long time ago's information could be passed all the way**.

The next two gates is to decide what new information we're going to store in the cell state. It is called **memory cell**.
Essentially, it will output C(t), where C(t) = gate_f(t) * C(t-1) + some_functio_of(h(t-1), x(t))

The right-bottom last gate called **output gate** decides what is our output h(t).

So essentially, a LSTM cell takes an input and stores it for some period of time. This is equivalent to applying the **identity function** to the input. **Because the derivative of the identity function is constant, when an LSTM network is trained with backpropagation through time, the gradient does NOT vanish**.

The activation function of the LSTM gates is often the logistic function. Intuitively, the input gate controls the extent to which a new value flows into the cell, the forget gate controls the extent to which a value remains in the cell, and the output gate controls the extent to which the value in the cell is used to compute the output activation of the LSTM unit.

There are connections into and out of the LSTM gates, a few of which are recurrent. The weights of these connections, which need to be learned during training, determine how the gates operate.

Important

LSTM has Turing completeness in the sense that given enough network units, it can compute any result that a conventional computer can compute, provided it has the proper weight matrix, which may be viewed as its program.

As you can see, LSTM is much complicated than a vanilla RNN.

One disadvantage of LSTM is: it is much slower than other normal activation functions, such as sigmoid, tanh or rectified linear unit.

9.5 Gated recurrent unit (GRU)

GRU is another popular RNN gating mechanism, introduced in 2014 by Kyunghyun Cho et al. It has been shown to exhibit better performance on smaller datasets, and has fewer parameters than LSTM.

The architecture is shown in the following diagram:

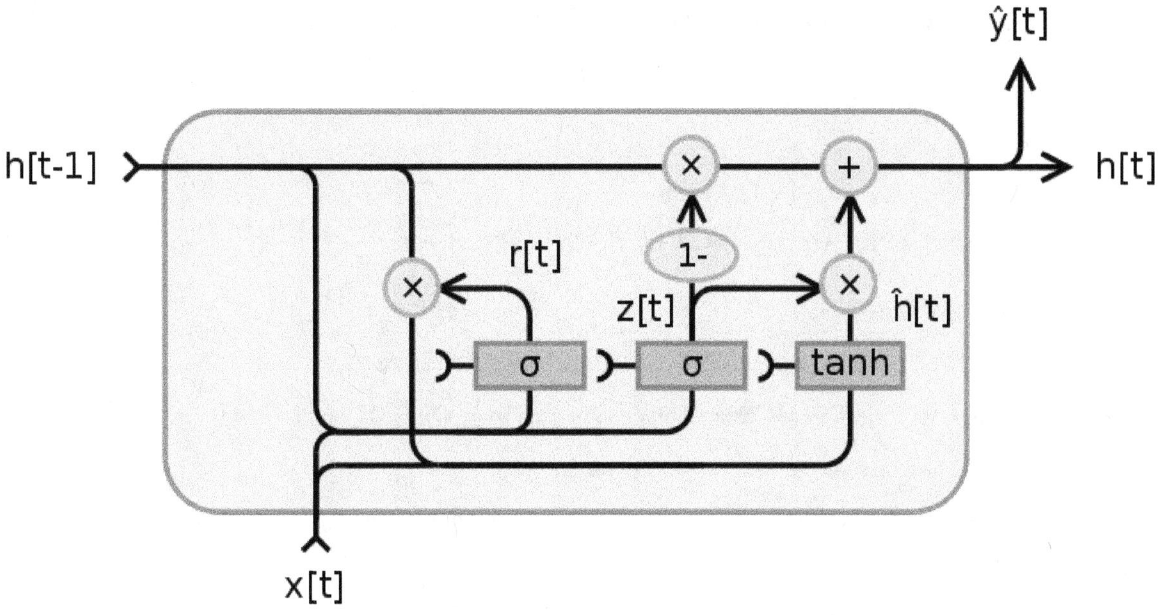

Figure 9.5: GRU architecture

Please note there are many variants of LSTMs, GRUs, RNNs.

One general issue of those RNNs(LSTM, GRU, valina RNNs) is that they are NOT hardware friendly, taking a lot of resources.

I will not spend much time on those details.

Interesting readers could find more information at:

https://en.wikipedia.org/wiki/Gated_recurrent_unit

https://en.wikipedia.org/wiki/Long_short-term_memory

http://karpathy.github.io/2015/05/21/rnn-effectiveness/

https://en.wikipedia.org/wiki/Residual_neural_network

http://www.wildml.com/2016/01/attention-and-memory-in-deep-learning-and-nlp/

http://colah.github.io/posts/2015-08-Understanding-LSTMs/

https://machinelearningmastery.com/when-to-use-mlp-cnn-and-rnn-neural-networks/

9.6 How to use/choose RNN/LSTM/GRU in pytorch

Pytorch supports three different types of RNNs.

According to:

https://pytorch.org/docs/stable/nn.html#rnn

It supports RNN, LSTM, GRU, RNNCell GRUCell, LSTMCell etc.

- **RNN** is the vanilla RNN.
- **GRU, LSTM** are just the regular GRU, LSTM we explained before.
- **RNNCell, GRUCell, LSTMCell** are cell classes used by RNN, GRU, and LSTM layer.
- RNN, GRU has the same API interface in pytorch.
- LSTM has a similar API interface as RNN, GRU, except it will output cell state.

9.7 how to understand seq_lens, batch_size, hidden size in pytorch RNN API

Now let's construct a RNN/GRU/LSTM using pytorch RNN API, as shown in the following code:

```
import torch
import torch.nn as nn
import torch.nn.functional as F
import torch.optim as optim
import torchvision
from torchvision import datasets, transforms

input_size = 28
hidden_size = 150
num_layers = 1

rnn = nn.RNN(input_size, hidden_size, num_layers)
gru = nn.GRU(input_size, hidden_size, num_layers)
lstm = nn.LSTM(input_size, hidden_size, num_layers)
```

Where:

- input_size – The number of expected features in the input x,
- hidden_size – The number of features in the hidden state h,
- num_layers – Number of recurrent layers. E.g., setting num_layers=2 would mean stacking two LSTMs together to form a stacked LSTM, with the second LSTM taking in outputs of the first LSTM and computing the final results. Default: 1

There are some additional parameters you can check online documents at:
https://pytorch.org/docs/stable/nn.html#rnn

Once we construct a RNN, we can feed data into it:

```
# timesteps
seq_len = 28
#
batch_size = 50
#
# input_size as previous one: 28

# input dat
input = torch.randn(seq_len, batch_size, input_size)

# initial hidden state
#   (num_layers * num_directions, batch_size, hidden_size)
h0 = torch.randn(1*1, batch_size, hidden_size)
c0 = torch.randn(1*1, batch_size, hidden_size)

# for rnn
output, hn = rnn(input, h0)

# for gru
output, hn = gru(input, h0)

# for lstm
output, (hn, cn) = lstm(input, (h0, c0))
```

For input:

- input of shape (seq_len, batch_size, input_size): tensor containing the features of the input sequence. The input can also be a packed variable length sequence. See torch.nn.utils.rnn.pack_padded_sequence() for details.
- h_0 of shape (num_layers * num_directions, batch_size, hidden_size): tensor containing the initial hidden state for each element in the batch. Defaults to zero if not provided. If the RNN is bidirectional, num_directions should be 2, else it should be 1. The seq_len sometimes is called as time steps as well.

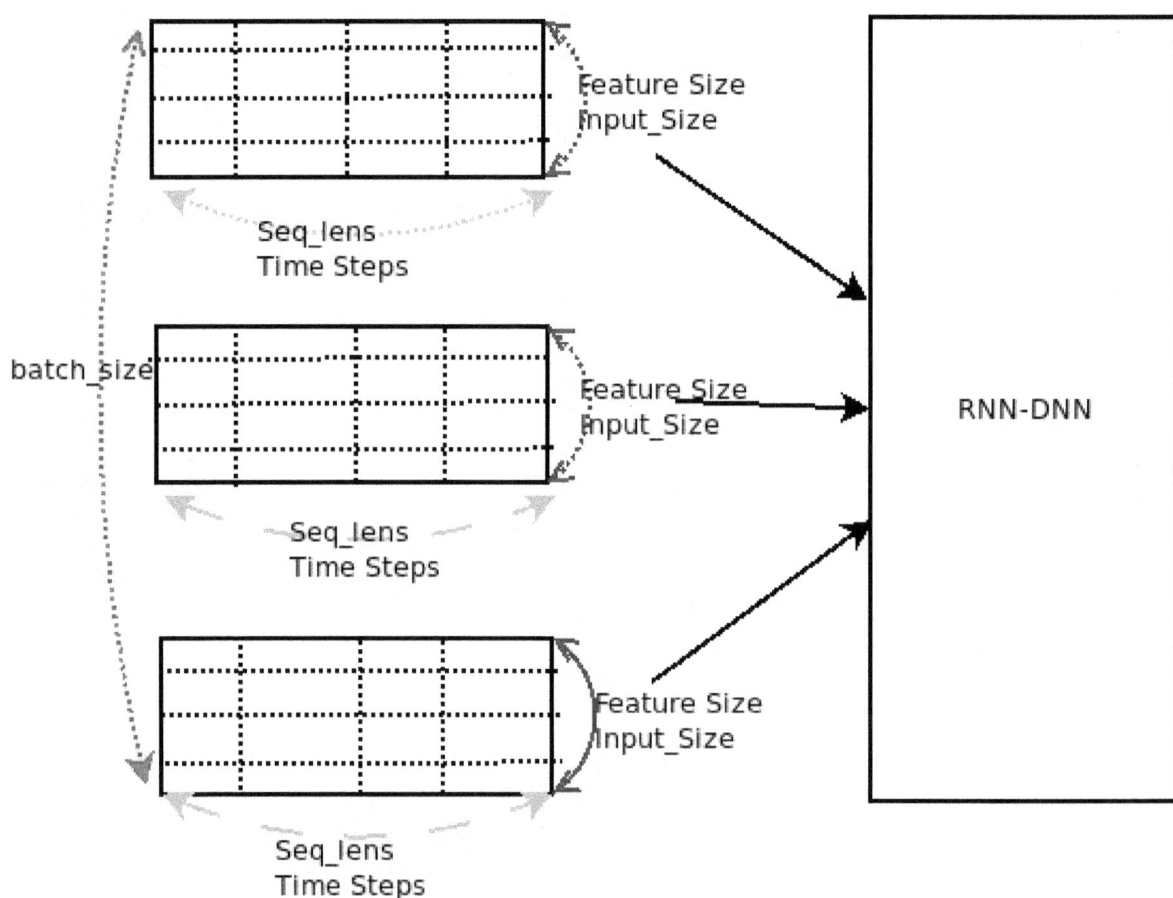

Figure 9.6: pytorch input to RNN

As shown in the figure above, assuming each little cell has some data. We can imagine input to RNN operates like the following:

- we feed batch_size samples into the system.
- for each example, we feed the data one by one with seq_len time steps,
- for each time_step, the data has input_size dimension, that means it has input_size features.

After all losses of batch_size samples got calculated, we updated gradient. That is the meaning of batch: We do not update gradient for each example, instead we sum and avg all batch_size samples.

Assume we have multiple layers of RNN stacked together, once data is fed into the initial layer of RNN, it will generate the outputs as the following figure:

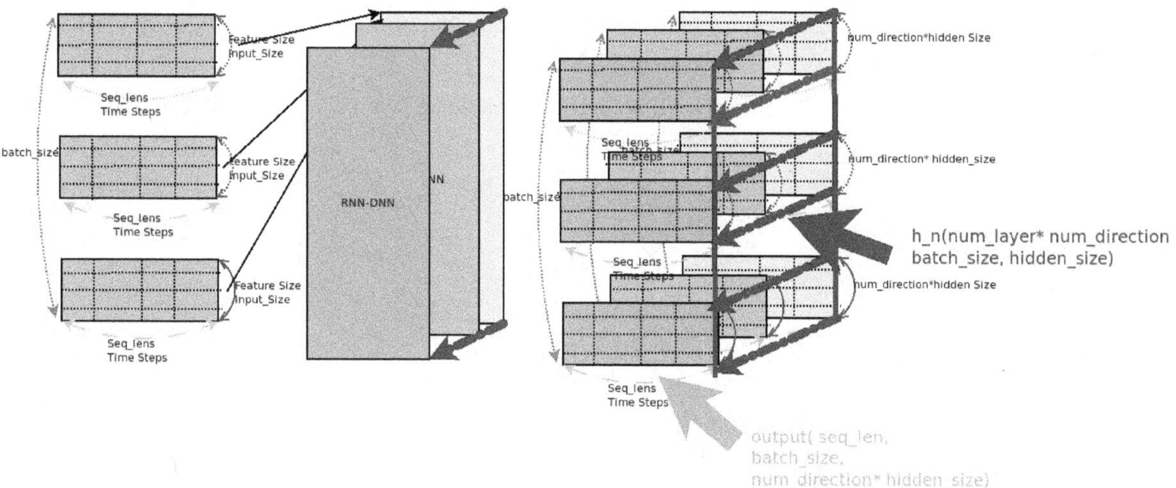

Figure 9.7: pytorch output from RNN

- output: it contains the output features h_t from the last layer of the RNN, for each t. The shape of output is: (seq_len, batch, num_directions * hidden_size). It is shown in the figure as yellow layer.
- h_n: it is a hidden state for t = seq_len, with shape (num_layers * num_directions, batch, hidden_size) It is shown in the figure as blue layer.

- c_n: it is only valid for LSTM, and contains cell state for t = seq_len, with the shape of: (num_layers * num_directions, batch, hidden_size). It is quite similar to h_n as far as shape looks.

The figure above clearly shows that RNN's outputs are most outside layer from that cube.

If we have just one non-bidirectional RNN layer, the h_n is actually equal to the output's last time step.

9.8 RNN classification example: MNIST again

If you look at our previous figure about the pytorch input and output for a while, you may have a feeling that the input is similar to some image data.

Yes, actually, we can treat an image using RNN!

Let's use MNIST data as an example, each MNIST image is 28x28, we can treat the first dimension of 28 as 28 time steps, while the second dimension as input feature.

Once we get the hidden state from RNN, we can feed it into a linear layer, the linear layer can be used as a classifier.

Here is the code:

```
# sample code for RNN to classify MNIST data
import torch
import torch.nn as nn
import torch.nn.functional as F
import torch.optim as optim
import torchvision
from torchvision import datasets, transforms

# MNIST data is 28x28
# instead of using CNN, we can actually try RNN as well:
# the first 28 can be thought as time steps
# the second 28 can be thought as input features
N_STEPS = 28
N_INPUTS = 28
# This is internal hidden_size for our RNN
N_NEURONS = 150
# final output since MNIST has 10 classes
N_OUTPUTS = 10
N_EPHOCS = 10
```

```

# a RNN class
class ImageRNN(nn.Module):
    def __init__(self, batch_size, n_steps, n_inputs, n_neurons, n_outputs):
        super(ImageRNN, self).__init__()
        self.n_neurons = n_neurons
        self.batch_size = batch_size
        # time steps: 28
        self.n_steps = n_steps
        self.n_inputs = n_inputs
        self.n_outputs = n_outputs
        # RNN input size: 28, hidden_size : 150
        self.basic_rnn = nn.RNN(self.n_inputs, self.n_neurons)
        # we output 10 classes
        self.FC = nn.Linear(self.n_neurons, self.n_outputs)

    def init_hidden(self,):
        # (num_layers, batch_size, n_neurons)
        return (torch.zeros(1, self.batch_size, self.n_neurons))

    def forward(self, X):
        # the original input is: batch_size x n_steps x n_inputs
        # as RNN need: (seq_len, batch_size, input_size):
        # so we use permute to
        # transforms X to new shape: n_steps X batch_size X n_inputs
        # permute (1,0,2) means
        # new data in dimension 0 comes from original dimension 1 etc.
        # thus (0,1,2) => (1, 0, 2)
        X = X.permute(1, 0, 2)

        self.batch_size = X.size(1)
        self.hidden = self.init_hidden()
        # now feed into rnn
        lstm_out, self.hidden = self.basic_rnn(X, self.hidden)
        # we use hidden layer as input to the last linear layer
        out = self.FC(self.hidden)
        # finally output as  10 classes
        return out.view(-1, self.n_outputs) # batch_size X n_output

# set our batch size
BATCH_SIZE = 64
# transform
```

```
transform = transforms.Compose( [ transforms.ToTensor(),
                                  transforms.Normalize((0.1307,), (0.3081,)) ] )
# save download location
data_dir="../data"

# download and load training dataset
trainset = torchvision.datasets.MNIST(root=data_dir, train=True,
                                      download=True, transform=transform)

trainloader = torch.utils.data.DataLoader(trainset, batch_size=BATCH_SIZE,
                                          shuffle=True, num_workers=2)

# download and load testing dataset
testset = torchvision.datasets.MNIST(root=data_dir, train=False,
                                     download=True, transform=transform)
testloader = torch.utils.data.DataLoader(testset, batch_size=BATCH_SIZE,
                                         shuffle=False, num_workers=2)


# just try to load one sample data
dataiter = iter(trainloader)
images, labels = dataiter.next()
model = ImageRNN(BATCH_SIZE, N_STEPS, N_INPUTS, N_NEURONS, N_OUTPUTS)
logits = model(images.view(-1, 28,28))
print(logits[0:10])

# Device
device = torch.device("cuda:0" if torch.cuda.is_available() else "cpu")

# Model instance
model = ImageRNN(BATCH_SIZE, N_STEPS, N_INPUTS, N_NEURONS, N_OUTPUTS)
criterion = nn.CrossEntropyLoss()
optimizer = optim.Adam(model.parameters(), lr=0.001)

def get_accuracy(logit, target, batch_size):
    ''' Obtain accuracy for training round '''
    corrects = (torch.max(logit, 1)[1].view(target.size()).data == target.data). ↩
        sum()
    accuracy = 100.0 * corrects/batch_size
    return accuracy.item()

# Training process
```

```
for epoch in range(N_EPHOCS):  # loop over the dataset multiple times
    train_running_loss = 0.0
    train_acc = 0.0
    # set model into training mode
    model.train()

    # TRAINING ROUND
    for i, data in enumerate(trainloader):
         # zero the parameter gradients
        optimizer.zero_grad()

        # reset hidden states
        model.hidden = model.init_hidden()

        # get the inputs
        inputs, labels = data
        # inputs will become (batch, h , w) e.g: 64 x 28 x 28
        inputs = inputs.view(-1, 28,28)

        # forward + backward + optimize
        outputs = model(inputs)

        loss = criterion(outputs, labels)
        loss.backward()
        optimizer.step()

        # add loss for this run
        train_running_loss += loss.detach().item()
        train_acc += get_accuracy(outputs, labels, BATCH_SIZE)

    # trained for this epoch
    print('Epoch:  %d | Loss: %.4f | Train Accuracy: %.2f'
          %(epoch, train_running_loss / i, train_acc/i))


# now let's evaluate on test data
test_acc = 0.0
# set model into evaluation mode
model.eval()

for i, data in enumerate(testloader, 0):
    inputs, labels = data
```

```
    inputs = inputs.view(-1, 28, 28)
    outputs = model(inputs)
    test_acc += get_accuracy(outputs, labels, BATCH_SIZE)

print('Test Accuracy: %.2f'%( test_acc/i))
```

Tip

You can download the complete code of this example from the author's repo (https://github.com/mingewang/pytorch_deep_learning_by_example) at: rnn/mnist_rnn.py

---

Power by the knowledge from the previous chapter, the code should be easy to understand.

Let's run it:

```
(pytorch-cpu) $ python mnist_rnn.py
tensor([[ 0.0325,  0.1215,  0.0026, -0.1089, -0.0751,  0.1095,  0.1412,  0.0741,
         -0.0645,  0.0175],
        [ 0.0802,  0.1373, -0.0138, -0.1258,  0.0268,  0.0013,  0.0945,  0.0847,
         -0.1088, -0.0073],
        [ 0.0420,  0.1270,  0.0371, -0.1132, -0.0622,  0.1528,  0.1406,  0.1014,
         -0.0460,  0.0723],
        [ 0.0215,  0.1181,  0.0006, -0.1290, -0.0806,  0.1060,  0.1375,  0.0741,
         -0.0636,  0.0051],
        [ 0.0403,  0.1672,  0.1527, -0.0889, -0.0756,  0.1562,  0.0739,  0.1389,
         -0.0716, -0.0186],
        [ 0.0621,  0.1407,  0.0563, -0.1684, -0.0363,  0.2056,  0.1164,  0.0641,
         -0.1044,  0.0663],
        [ 0.0138,  0.1113,  0.0313, -0.1156, -0.0807,  0.1303,  0.1187,  0.0642,
         -0.0343,  0.0121],
        [ 0.0258,  0.1208,  0.0078, -0.1085, -0.0800,  0.1083,  0.1375,  0.0677,
         -0.0674,  0.0059],
        [ 0.0279,  0.1155,  0.0254, -0.1159, -0.0782,  0.1343,  0.1381,  0.0935,
         -0.0392,  0.0420],
        [ 0.0219,  0.1193,  0.0226, -0.1169, -0.0816,  0.1090,  0.1114,  0.0682,
         -0.0473,  0.0105]], grad_fn=<SliceBackward>)
Epoch:  0 | Loss: 0.6521 | Train Accuracy: 78.53
Epoch:  1 | Loss: 0.2651 | Train Accuracy: 92.02
```

```
Epoch:  2 | Loss: 0.2033 | Train Accuracy: 93.87
Epoch:  3 | Loss: 0.1679 | Train Accuracy: 94.86
Epoch:  4 | Loss: 0.1477 | Train Accuracy: 95.41
Epoch:  5 | Loss: 0.1366 | Train Accuracy: 95.70
Epoch:  6 | Loss: 0.1322 | Train Accuracy: 95.88
Epoch:  7 | Loss: 0.1207 | Train Accuracy: 96.21
Epoch:  8 | Loss: 0.1215 | Train Accuracy: 96.15
Epoch:  9 | Loss: 0.1133 | Train Accuracy: 96.41
Test Accuracy: 96.68
```

We got 96.68% accuracy, not bad!

9.9 RNN generative model: a text generate example

RNN can be used not only in predictive models (making predictions), but also in generative models. We can use it to generate text, music, video etc.

Pytorch provides a good example of how to generate text at:

https://pytorch.org/tutorials/intermediate/char_rnn_generation_tutorial.html

It showed how to use linear layer to build an RNN instead of using pytorch build-in RNN/LSTM layer.

The following example, however, will show you how to use pytorch build-in RNN/LSTM layer directly.

The main idea is similar to any other text generation RNN: we train our model to predict the next char from the previous sequence seen before.

Let's look at the code. Yes, please do read the code, even better to run it on google's colab or your local environment, thus you will have a much better understanding of RNN.

Tip

You can download the complete code of this example from the author's repo (https://github.com/mingewang/pytorch_deep_learning_by_example) at: rnn/pytorch_lstm_text_generate.py

```
# sample code for text generate using RNN/lstm
import torch
```

```
import torch.nn as nn
import torch.nn.functional as F
import torch.optim as optim
import torchvision
from torchvision import datasets, transforms
from torch.utils.data import Dataset
from torchvision.datasets.utils import download_url

import numpy as np
import random
import sys
import io
import os

# a class for Text generate using LSTM
class TextRNN(nn.Module):
    def __init__(self, batch_size, n_steps, n_inputs, n_neurons, n_outputs):
        super(TextRNN, self).__init__()
        self.n_neurons = n_neurons
        self.batch_size = batch_size
        # time steps: max_length for text
        self.n_steps = n_steps
        self.n_inputs = n_inputs
        self.n_outputs = n_outputs
        # RNN input feature size: , hidden_size : 128
        self.basic_rnn = nn.LSTM(self.n_inputs, self.n_neurons)
        # we output feature size should be the same as input feature size
        # we need to use one-hot in RNN class, but not in data
        self.FC = nn.Linear(self.n_neurons, self.n_outputs)

    # lstm need: h_n, c_n
    def init_hidden(self):
        # (num_layers, batch_size, n_neurons)
        return (torch.zeros(1, self.batch_size, self.n_neurons), torch.zeros(1, ↩
            self.batch_size, self.n_neurons))

    def forward(self, X):
        # the original input is: batch_size x n_steps x n_inputs
        # as RNN need: (seq_len, batch_size, input_size):
        # so we use permute to
        # transforms X to new shape: n_steps X batch_size X n_inputs
        # permute (1,0,2) means
```

```
        # new data in dimension 0 comes from original dimension 1 etc.
        # thus (0,1,2) => (1, 0, 2)
        X = X.permute(1, 0, 2)

        # in case batch_size changed
        self.batch_size = X.size(1)

        self.hidden, self.cn = self.init_hidden()
        # by default those tensor are on cpu
        # let's sync hidden, cn to the same device as X
        device = X.device
        self.hidden, self.cn = self.hidden.to(device), self.cn.to(device)

        # now feed into rnn
        lstm_out,(self.hidden, self.cn) = self.basic_rnn(X, (self.hidden, self.cn))
        # we use hidden layer as input to the last linear layer
        out = self.FC(self.hidden)
        # finally output as output dimension's classes
        out =  out.view(-1, self.n_outputs) # batch_size X n_output
        return F.log_softmax(out, dim=1) # batch_size X n_output

# write a dataset to prepare data
class TextDataset(Dataset):
  def __init__(self, root_dir, url, maxlen, download=False, transform=None):
    self.root_dir = root_dir
    self.transform = transform
    filename = "tmp_text_dataset.txt"

    if download:
      download_url(url, root_dir, filename, md5=None)

    path = os.path.join(root_dir, filename)
    with io.open(path, encoding='utf-8') as f:
        text = f.read().lower()

    #replace \n with space
    text=text.replace('\n',' ')
    print('corpus length:', len(text))

    # that will be our input/output features
    chars = sorted(list(set(text)))
```

```
        print('total chars:', len(chars))
        # convert chars to integer category
        char_indices = dict((c, i) for i, c in enumerate(chars))
        indices_char = dict((i, c) for i, c in enumerate(chars))


        # cut the text in semi-redundant sequences of maxlen characters
        self.maxlen = maxlen #40
        step = 1
        sentences = []
        next_chars = []
        # we prepare input and target output
        # we use input[i:i+maxlen1] to predict output[i + maxlen]
        for i in range(0, len(text) - maxlen, step):
            # i is the sample index
            # sentences contains the sample input
            # next_chars contains the target output
            sentences.append(text[i: i + maxlen])
            next_chars.append(text[i + maxlen])
        print('number of sequences:', len(sentences))

        print('Vectorization...')
        # one-hot vector for input: from first to last letter ( max_len)
        x = torch.zeros(len(sentences), maxlen, len(chars) )
        # should just be the predicted next char after max_len,
        y = torch.zeros(len(sentences), dtype=torch.long )
        for i, sentence in enumerate(sentences):
            for t, char in enumerate(sentence):
                x[i, t, char_indices[char]] = 1
            #y[i, char_indices[next_chars[i]]] = 1
            y[i] = char_indices[next_chars[i]]
        print('Vectorization done')

        # store the mapping for future sampling
        self.chars = chars
        self.char_indices = char_indices
        self.indices_char = indices_char
        # convert x, y to tensor from numpy
        self.x = x
        self.y = y

    # size of the whole dataset
```

```
  def __len__(self):
    return len(self.x)

  def __getitem__(self, idx):
    item_x = self.x[idx]
    item_y = self.y[idx]

    if self.transform:
        item_x = self.transform(item_x)
        item_y = self.transform(item_y)

    return item_x, item_y

  # help function
  def input_feature_size(self):
    return len(self.chars)

  # same as input feature
  def output_feature_size(self):
    return len(self.chars)

  def convert_index_to_char(self, char_index):
    char = self.indices_char[char_index]
    return char

  def convert_char_to_index(self, char):
    char_index = self.char_indices[char]
    return char_index

# # cut the text in semi-redundant sequences of maxlen characters
N_STEPS = 40
# This is internal hidden_size for our RNN
N_NEURONS = 128
N_EPHOCS = 60
# set our batch size
BATCH_SIZE = 64

max_len = N_STEPS

# download and load training dataset
url='http://www.cs.cmu.edu/afs/cs/project/ai-repository/ai/areas/nlp/corpora/ ↩
   names/male.txt'
```

```
root_dir = "./data"
# transform
#transform = transforms.Compose( [ transforms.ToTensor() ] )
trainset = TextDataset(root_dir, url, max_len )
trainloader = torch.utils.data.DataLoader(trainset, batch_size=BATCH_SIZE,
                                          shuffle=True, num_workers=2)

# the input feature depends on the text we downloaded
N_INPUTS = trainset.input_feature_size()
# final output's feature dimension is the same as input dimension
N_OUTPUTS = trainset.output_feature_size()
# for simplicity reason, no test set

# just try to load one sample data
dataiter = iter(trainloader)
text_x, labels = dataiter.next()
#print("text_x is: ", text_x, " labels is: ", labels)
print("text_x is: ", text_x.shape, " labels is: ", labels.shape)

model = TextRNN(BATCH_SIZE, N_STEPS, N_INPUTS, N_NEURONS, N_OUTPUTS)
#logits = model(text_x.view(-1, N_STEPS, N_INPUTS))
logits = model(text_x)

#print(logits[0:10])
print("output shape:", logits.shape)

# Device
device = torch.device("cuda:0" if torch.cuda.is_available() else "cpu")

# save our model here
model_saved_filename = "lstm_text_trained.model"

def get_accuracy(logit, target, batch_size):
    ''' Obtain accuracy for training round '''
    corrects = (torch.max(logit, 1)[1].view(target.size()).data == target.data). ↩
        sum()
    accuracy = 100.0 * corrects/batch_size
    return accuracy.item()

def train():
  # Model instance
  model = TextRNN(BATCH_SIZE, N_STEPS, N_INPUTS, N_NEURONS, N_OUTPUTS)
```

```

    # put model into that GPU or CPU
    model = model.to(device)

    criterion = nn.CrossEntropyLoss()
    optimizer = optim.Adam(model.parameters(), lr=0.001)

    # Training process
    for epoch in range(N_EPHOCS):  # loop over the dataset multiple times
        train_running_loss = 0.0
        train_acc = 0.0
        # set model into training mode
        model.train()

        # TRAINING ROUND, get one batch of data
        for i, data in enumerate(trainloader):
             # zero the parameter gradients
            optimizer.zero_grad()

            # reset hidden states
            model.hidden = model.init_hidden()

            # get the inputs,
            # inputs will become (batch, N_STPES , N_INPUTS) e.g: 64 x 40 x len( ↩
                chars)
            inputs, labels = data
            # data is python list, where inputs, labels are tensors
            # put data into that device: GPU or CPU
            inputs, labels = inputs.to(device), labels.to(device)
            # inputs will become (batch, h , w) e.g: 64 x 28 x 28
            # inputs = inputs.view(-1, N_STEPS, N_INPUTS)

            # forward + backward + optimize
            outputs = model(inputs)

            loss = criterion(outputs, labels)
            loss.backward()
            optimizer.step()

            # add loss for this run
            train_running_loss += loss.detach().item()
            train_acc += get_accuracy(outputs, labels, BATCH_SIZE)
```

```
        # trained for this epoch
        print('Epoch:  %d | Loss: %.4f | Train Accuracy: %.2f'
              %(epoch, train_running_loss / i, train_acc/i))

        # save model
        torch.save(model.state_dict(), model_saved_filename)


def generate_text(model, dataset, maxlen,seed_text):
    print('----- Generating text')
    generated = ''
    sentence = seed_text
    generated += sentence
    print('----- Generating with seed: "' + sentence + '"')

    input_feature_size = dataset.input_feature_size()

    for i in range(400):
        # sample sentence input
        x_pred = torch.zeros(1, maxlen, input_feature_size)
        # one-hot encode previous sentence
        for t, char in enumerate(sentence):
            char_index = dataset.convert_char_to_index(char)
            x_pred[0, t, char_index] = 1.
        # feed to model
        #import pdb
        #pdb.set_trace()
        # feed sentence into our model to predict next char
        output = model(x_pred)
        # here we just choose top 1,
        #topv is the prob, topi is the index
        topv, topi = output.topk(1)
        topi = topi[0][0]
        next_index = topi.item()
        # convert char_index into char
        next_char = dataset.convert_index_to_char(next_index)

        # append to our generated text
        generated += next_char
        # move/shift sentence to next one for the next round of prediction
        sentence = sentence[1:] + next_char
```

```
292        print('----- Final text: "' + generated + '"')
293
294
295    train()
296
297    # load saved model
298    model = TextRNN(BATCH_SIZE, N_STEPS, N_INPUTS, N_NEURONS, N_OUTPUTS)
299    model.load_state_dict(torch.load(model_saved_filename))
300    model.eval()
301    generate_text(model, trainset, max_len, "her christorpher christos christy chrisy ↩
           ")
```

- Line 18 - 63, we define a TextRNN model. It is quite similar to previous MNIST RNN example. The difference between LSTM and RNN/GRU is LSTM outputs not only hidden state, but also cell state. Thus we need to update cell state accordingly.
- Line 52 - 55, we use a small trick to make TextRNN more friendly to be used on GPU (cuda) by syncing the initial hidden state/cell_state on the device as input X.
- Line 66 - 154, we implement a dataset to download a text from an URL. The dataset interface is quite simple, we just need to implement __len *and__getitem*, the rest of them are just some helper functions.
- Line 66- 124, the main purpose of those codes is to pre-process data.

The codes are adopted from keras lstm_text_generation.py example.

- Line 68 - 77, we use the pytorch built-in download_url to download a file from a URL, then we load the content of that file into "text".
- Line 80 - 88, we find all unique chars, then assign each char an integer index, and store those mapping for later use.
- Line 91 - 104, we prepare many training examples, for each example, it has a sentence of max_len long as input and its next char as target for our future training.
- Line 108 - 116, we one-hot encode the input as DNN only accept that. But we do NOT need to one-hot encode target, as pytorch loss function expect a class index (integer) instead of one-hot vector for that label. **That is one difference from keras in case you are have keras background**.
- Line 119 - 134, we store those info.

- Line 129 - 138, we implement the standard Dataset interface.
- Line 141 - 192, we define some helper functions.
- Line 197 - 214, we define some parameters, helper function, etc like previous MNIST example, then create a TextDateSet instance, and dataloader instance etc.
- Line 206 - 256, we specify how we train the data. It is quite similar to the previous MNIST example as well. The only difference is we save the model at Line 256 using torch.save and model.state_dict().
- Line 259 - 292, we showed how to generate text using the trained model. The idea is simple: we prepare a max_len sentence with some initial seed chars, then we feed this sentence into the model to get the next char (predicted char from the model), now, we append this char to the sentence to construct a new max_len sentence (just shift one char as shown in Line 291), this new sentence will be used to predict the next char, we can keep on looping on this process to generate more chars.
- Line 282 - 284, we just pick the top 1 prediction as the next char simply for the demo purpose. As you can image, we can make it fancier by picking the top 2 or 3, or in some creative ways.
- Line 298 - 301, we showed how to load a pre-trained model by using model.load_state_dict, and torch.load.

In this example, I just use a very small data set file, so that we can easily see the result. Specifically, we will train a lstm network to generate a boy's name.

You can easily modify the URL to try other files.

As LSTM (in general RNN) is quite computationally intensive, it is recommended to run this script on GPU.

I just copy/paste the code into google's colab with GPU run-time enabled, and here is the result:

```
Epoch:  0 | Loss: 2.9493 | Train Accuracy: 14.99
Epoch:  1 | Loss: 2.5876 | Train Accuracy: 24.34
Epoch:  2 | Loss: 2.4299 | Train Accuracy: 27.07
Epoch:  3 | Loss: 2.3125 | Train Accuracy: 30.89
...
...
Epoch:  57 | Loss: 0.1314 | Train Accuracy: 96.78
Epoch:  58 | Loss: 0.1424 | Train Accuracy: 96.26
Epoch:  59 | Loss: 0.1801 | Train Accuracy: 94.70

----- Generating text
----- Generating with seed: "her christorpher christos christy chrisy"
```

```
----- Final text: "her christorpher christos christy chrisy chuck churchill clair
 claie claybon clayborn claibore claibon llai tlin peller cen tevy cev
cevyton cevy chey chetchol chisthol kitth christophe chroston christy
christon churickich churlyy cyustiey cyb daid caid walet waleston waley
waxtary wayton way wayley wayler waylen waylen waylen waylen waylen waylen
waylen waylen waylen waylen waylen waylen waylen waylen waylen waylen waylen
waylen waylen"
```

The generated name is not bad, considering we have a very small dataset and such a simple LSTM network.

This example clearly showed the power of RNN/LSTM network, especially dealing with sequence data. Just use your imagination, you probably can use RNN to generate text, audio, video, etc, there is no limitation that RNN can not generate!

Some more interesting examples can be found at:
http://karpathy.github.io/2015/05/21/rnn-effectiveness/

9.10 When and how to use MLP, CNN, RNN

So far we have learned three fundamental building blocks of neural networks: MLP, CNN, RNN.

Many real-life projects need not just one type of building block, but several different types of blocks mixed together.

The question becomes which building block should we choose, and how to choose?

Here is some rule of thumb:

If we have image data, most likely, we will add some CNN layers. A one-dimensional CNN can sometimes be used to handle text/time series data.

If we have some sequence data such as text, speech/audio, video, etc, most likely, we will add some RNN layers.

If we want to generate something (a generative model), we may want to consider some RNN layers.

It is normal to add some MLP layers (in keras normally called dense layer), dropout, embedding layers, etc.

9.11 summary

In this chapter, we have learned why, where, and how to use RNN in pytorch.

In particular, you should know what are the differences among vanilla RNN, LSTM, GRU, and where/how to use them in different scenarios with pytorch API.

Congregations! Now with all the knowledge so far, we are ready to explore more interesting deep learning applications!

Chapter 10

How to deploy deep learning model

Let's say we spent lots of effort to design the model, train the model. At the end of the day, our final goal is to serve prediction requests from other systems, right?

But how?

In the chapter, I will show you how to write a simple Rest API, and how to deploy models using TorchServe.

10.1 Build your own REST API service

The most popular/useful way is to wrap service as a REST API service.

A very good illustrated example could be found at:
https://github.com/L1aoXingyu/deploy-pytorch-model

It just needs one file (run_keras_server.py) to wrap a pre-trained model as REST API.

It is based on:
https://github.com/jrosebr1/simple-keras-rest-api

I updated so it can run using pytorch 1.0 and put the change in a comrite branch at:
https://github.com/mingewang/deploy-pytorch-model

You can view the code at:
https://github.com/mingewang/deploy-pytorch-model/tree/comrite

Anyway, here is the run_pytorch_server:

```
# encoding: utf-8
"""
@author: xyliao
@contact: xyliao1993@qq.com
"""

import io
import json

import flask
import torch
import torch
import torch.nn.functional as F
from PIL import Image
from torch import nn
from torchvision import transforms as T
from torchvision.models import resnet50

# Initialize our Flask application and the PyTorch model.
app = flask.Flask(__name__)
model = None
device = torch.device('cuda' if torch.cuda.is_available() else 'cpu')
print('Using device:', device)
use_gpu = True if torch.cuda.is_available() else False

with open('imagenet_class.txt', 'r') as f:
    idx2label = eval(f.read())


def load_model():
    """Load the pre-trained model, you can use your model just as easily.

    """
    global model
    model = resnet50(pretrained=True)
    model.eval()
    if use_gpu:
        model.cuda()

```

```python

def prepare_image(image, target_size):
    """Do image preprocessing before prediction on any data.

    :param image:       original image
    :param target_size: target image size
    :return:
                        preprocessed image
    """

    if image.mode != 'RGB':
        image = image.convert("RGB")

    # Resize the input image and preprocess it.
    image = T.Resize(target_size)(image)
    image = T.ToTensor()(image)

    # Convert to Torch.Tensor and normalize.
    image = T.Normalize([0.485, 0.456, 0.406], [0.229, 0.224, 0.225])(image)

    # Add batch_size axis.
    image = image[None]
    if use_gpu:
        image = image.cuda()
    return torch.autograd.Variable(image, volatile=True)


@app.route("/predict", methods=["POST"])
def predict():
    # Initialize the data dictionary that will be returned from the view.
    data = {"success": False}

    # Ensure an image was properly uploaded to our endpoint.
    if flask.request.method == 'POST':
        if flask.request.files.get("image"):
            # Read the image in PIL format
            image = flask.request.files["image"].read()
            image = Image.open(io.BytesIO(image))

            # Preprocess the image and prepare it for classification.
            image = prepare_image(image, target_size=(224, 224))

```

```
82              # Classify the input image and then initialize the list of predictions to return to the client.
83              preds = F.softmax(model(image), dim=1)
84              results = torch.topk(preds.cpu().data, k=3, dim=1)
85
86              data['predictions'] = list()
87
88              # Loop over the results and add them to the list of returned predictions
89              for prob, label in zip(results[0][0], results[1][0]):
90                  label_name = idx2label[label.item()]
91                  r = {"label": label_name, "probability": float(prob)}
92                  data['predictions'].append(r)
93
94              # Indicate that the request was a success.
95              data["success"] = True
96
97      # Return the data dictionary as a JSON response.
98      return flask.jsonify(data)
99
100
101 if __name__ == '__main__':
102     print("Loading PyTorch model and Flask starting server ...")
103     print("Please wait until server has fully started")
104     load_model()
105     app.run()
```

The code above is quite clean with very nice inline documents, so should be easy to understand.

It uses the neat flask as web/REST API server,

- Line 34-38, just load the model before serving the request.
- Line 105, start the app to service the predict request.
- Line 68 - 98 handles the predict request, while Line 83 call the model to do the prediction.

Let's run it as the following:

```
# need to go to install those pkgs
# pip install flask gevent requests
```

```

(pytorch-cpu) $ python run_pytorch_server.py
Using device: cpu
Loading PyTorch model and Flask starting server ...
Please wait until server has fully started
 * Serving Flask app "run_pytorch_server" (lazy loading)
 * Environment: production
   WARNING: Do not use the development server in a production environment.
   Use a production WSGI server instead.
 * Debug mode: off
 * Running on http://127.0.0.1:5000/ (Press CTRL+C to quit)
run_pytorch_server.py:64: UserWarning: volatile was removed and now has no effect ↩
    . Use 'with torch.no_grad():' instead.
  return torch.autograd.Variable(image, volatile=True)
```

Now, in another terminal, we can use curl to test it:

```
(pytorch-cpu) $ python simple_request.py --file='./dog.jpg'
1. beagle: 0.9503
2. Walker hound, Walker foxhound: 0.0321
3. English foxhound: 0.0035
```

This simple REST API server get you jump-started, however, it is single-threaded, can not serve concurrent requests.

A more scaled version could be looks like the following:

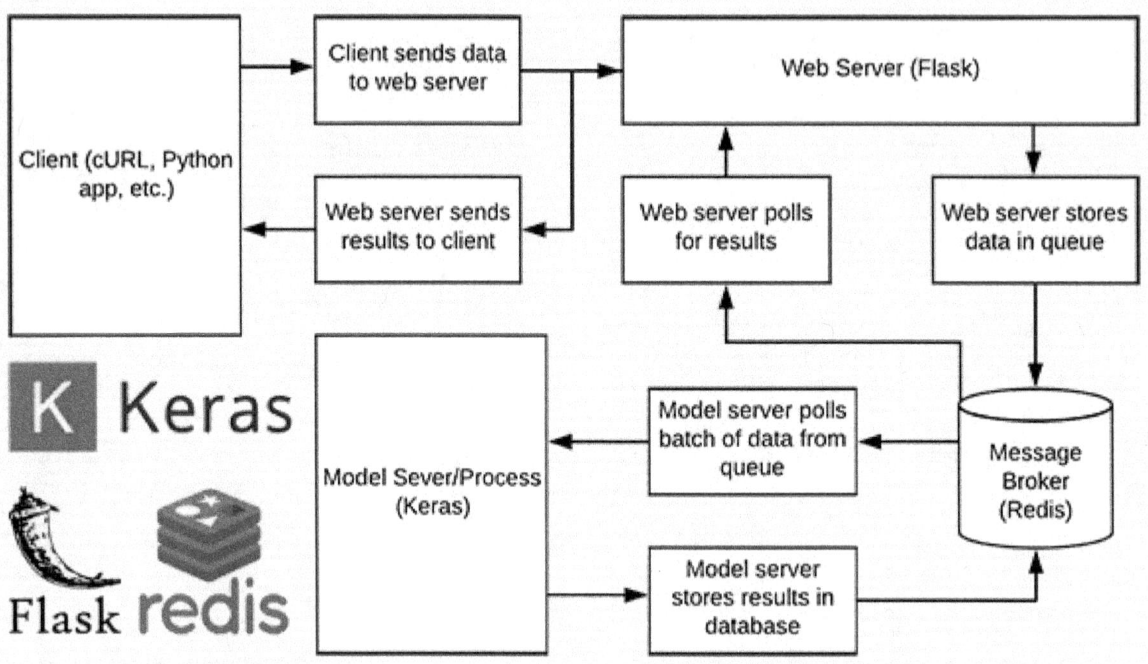

Figure 10.1: a scaled version of deep learning REST API server

The key concept there is to use Redis to queue the requests, and later on the model_server can grab batches of requests and predict in batch.

Please read more details at:
https://www.pyimagesearch.com/2018/02/05/deep-learning-production-keras-redis-flask-apache/

We should be able to use this architecture to wrap other deep learning frameworks (e.g.: Pytorch) as REST API services as well.

10.2 TorchServe

Around April, 2020, PyTorch introduced TorchServe, an open-source model serving library for PyTorch. With TorchServe, you can deploy PyTorch models in either eager or graph mode using TorchScript, serve multiple models simultaneously, version production models for A/B testing, load and unload models dynamically, and monitor detailed logs and customizable metrics.

Here is the architecture:

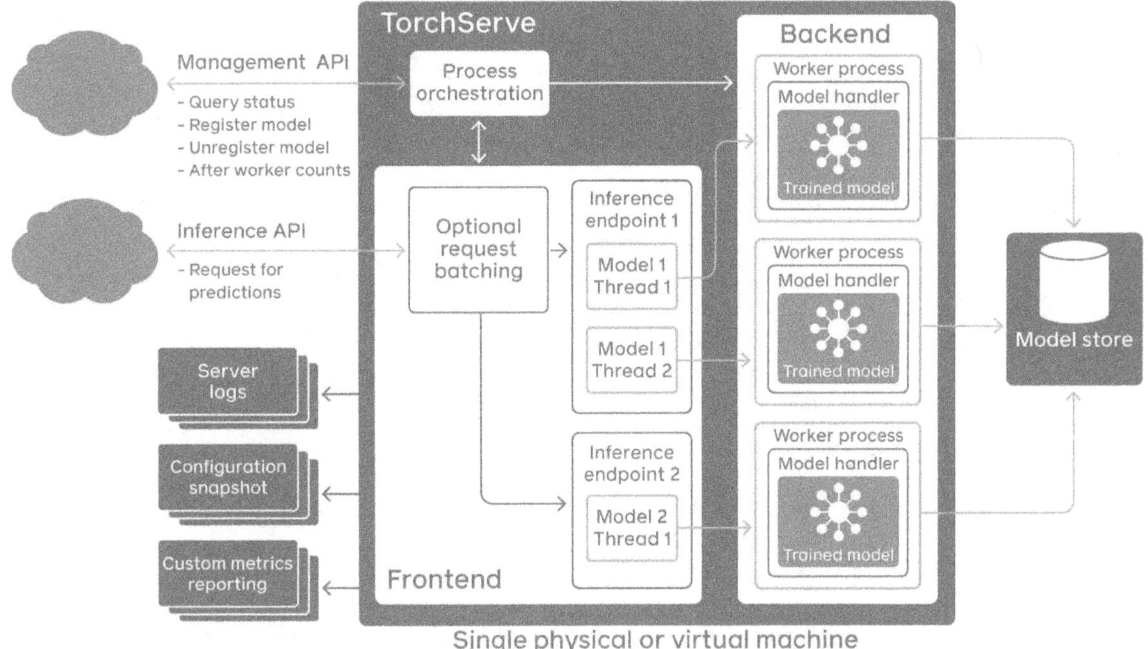

Figure 10.2: torch serve architecture

The basic idea is: we package model related artifacts into a single archive file (.mar format), then deploy it to TorchServe. The Torchserve system will serve the inference request automagically for us.

There are several ways to install/configure/deploy TorchServe as shown in the official document is at: https://github.com/pytorch/serve

Among them, the easier way is to use docker as shown in the document: https://github.com/pytorch/serve/blob/master/docker/README.md

In the section, I will use docker to deploy TorchServe.

10.2.1 torch-model-archiver : export model as .mar file

The first step is to export your model as .mar file using torch-model-archiver, which basically packages all model artifacts into a single model archive file.

Here is a sample procedure on how to do it using docker.

```
# pull torch serve docker image
$ docker pull pytorch/torchserve:latest

# you can use existing files from:
# https://github.com/mingewang/pytorch_deep_learning_by_example/tree/master/ ↩
    torch_serve
$ git clone https://github.com/mingewang/pytorch_deep_learning_by_example/
$ cd torch_serve

# mkdir -p torch_serve/model-store
cd torch_serve

# make a .mar file

# download densenet model
# we need to convert this model into .mar file
wget https://download.pytorch.org/models/densenet161-8d451a50.pth

# mount torch_serve as /home/test in the container
$ docker run --rm -it -v $(pwd):/home/test pytorch/torchserve /bin/bash

# inside the container, now convert the model into .mar file
model-server@d1909dbe9592 $  cd /home/test/

model-server@d1909dbe9592 $ torch-model-archiver --model-name densenet161 \
--version 1.0 --model-file ./model.py \
--serialized-file ./densenet161-8d451a50.pth \
--export-path ./model-store --extra-files ./index_to_name.json \
--handler image_classifier

# check the .mar generated
model-server@d1909dbe9592 $ ls -lh model_store/
total 106M
-rw-r--r-- 1 model-server model-server 106M Sep 20 18:20 densenet161.mar
```

```
# exit container
$ model-server@d1909dbe9592 $ exit
```

Torch-model-archiever need some input arguments, which should not be difficult to guess. The following showed the more detailed explanation.

```
rguments
$ torch-model-archiver -h
usage: torch-model-archiver [-h] --model-name MODEL_NAME  --version ↩
    MODEL_VERSION_NUMBER
                      --model-file MODEL_FILE_PATH --serialized-file ↩
                        MODEL_SERIALIZED_PATH
                      --handler HANDLER [--runtime {python,python2,python3}]
                      [--export-path EXPORT_PATH] [-f] [--requirements-file]

Model Archiver Tool

optional arguments:
  -h, --help            show this help message and exit
  --model-name MODEL_NAME
                        Exported model name. Exported file will be named as
                        model-name.mar and saved in current working directory
                        if no --export-path is specified, else it will be
                        saved under the export path
  --serialized-file SERIALIZED_FILE
                        Path to .pt or .pth file containing state_dict in
                        case of eager mode or an executable ScriptModule
                        in case of TorchScript.
  --model-file MODEL_FILE
                        Path to python file containing model architecture.
                        This parameter is mandatory for eager mode models.
                        The model architecture file must contain only one
                        class definition extended from torch.nn.modules.
  --handler HANDLER     TorchServe's default handler name  or handler python
                        file path to handle custom TorchServe inference logic.
  --extra-files EXTRA_FILES
                        Comma separated path to extra dependency files.
  --runtime {python,python2,python3}
                        The runtime specifies which language to run your
                        inference code on. The default runtime is
```

```
                        RuntimeType.PYTHON. At the present moment we support
                        the following runtimes python, python2, python3
  --export-path EXPORT_PATH
                        Path where the exported .mar file will be saved. This
                        is an optional parameter. If --export-path is not
                        specified, the file will be saved in the current
                        working directory.
  --archive-format {tgz,default}
                        The format in which the model artifacts are archived.
                        "tgz": This creates the model-archive in <model-name>.tar.gz format.
                        If platform hosting requires model-artifacts to be in ".tar.gz"
                        use this option.
                        "no-archive": This option creates an non-archived version of model artifacts
                        at "export-path/{model-name}" location. As a result of this choice,
                        MANIFEST file will be created at "export-path/{model-name}" location
                        without archiving these model files
                        "default": This creates the model-archive in <model-name>.mar format.
                        This is the default archiving format. Models archived in this format
                        will be readily hostable on TorchServe.
  -f, --force           When the -f or --force flag is specified, an existing
                        .mar file with same name as that provided in --model-
                        name in the path specified by --export-path will
                        overwritten
  -v, --version         Model's version.
  -r, -requirements-file
                        Path to requirements.txt file containing a list of model specific python
                        packages to be installed by TorchServe for seamless model serving.
```

You can read more documents at:
https://github.com/pytorch/serve/blob/master/model-archiver/README.md
https://github.com/pytorch/serve/tree/master/model-archiver#creating-a-model-archive

10.2.2 torch-serve : serve the model as .mar file

Once we got the .mar file, we can deploy it:

```
# run the torchserve
$ docker run --rm -it -v $(pwd)/model-store:/home/model-server/model-store \
-p 8080:8080 -p 8081:8081 pytorch/torchserve \
torchserve --start --ncs --model-store model-store --models densenet161.mar

# to load all models, pass the --models all
# https://github.com/pytorch/serve/blob/master/docs/configuration.md


# you should see similar like this:
$ 2020-09-20 11:02:58,097 [INFO ] main org.pytorch.serve.ModelServer -
Torchserve version: 0.2.0
...
Model server started.
..
```

The official document could be found at:
https://github.com/pytorch/serve/blob/master/docker/README.md

Now test it:

```
# download a sample image if do not have
#$ curl -O https://s3.amazonaws.com/model-server/inputs/kitten.jpg

# test it
$ curl http://127.0.0.1:8080/predictions/densenet161 -T kitten.jpg
{
  "tiger_cat": 0.4693339765071869,
  "tabby": 0.4633894264698028б,
  "Egyptian_cat": 0.0645614042878151,
  "lynx": 0.0012828147737309337,
  "plastic_bag": 0.00023323003551922739
}
```

Ah, it is working!

10.2.3 custom service, and custom handler

In our previous example of torch-model-archiver, we pass a default build-in handler.

What is the handler?
It short, the handler is responsible to make a prediction from one or more HTTP requests.

TorchServe supports following handlers out of the box: * image_classifier * object_detector * text_classifier * image_segmenter

More details at:
https://github.com/pytorch/serve/blob/master/docs/default_handlers.md

Sometimes, the default handlers may not work as we required, we need to have a custom handler to to handle the TorchServe inference logic for those cases.

TorchServe calls it custom service. which is responsible for handling incoming data and passing on to engine for inference. The output of the custom service is returned back as response by TorchServe.

How to write a custom handler?

We generally derive from BaseHandler and ONLY override methods whose behavior needs to change! Most of the time we only need to override preprocess or postprocess

The following code showed how to write a custom handler, please read through the code and its comments:

```
"""
Custom handler for pytorch serve.
reference documents:
https://pytorch.org/serve/custom_service.html
https://github.com/pytorch/serve/blob/master/docs/custom_service.md
https://github.com/FrancescoSaverioZuppichini/torchserve-tryout
"""
import logging
import torch
import torch.nn.functional as F
import io
from PIL import Image
from torchvision import transforms
from ts.torch_handler.base_handler import BaseHandler

# Custom handler with class level entry point
# The handler can extend from any of following:
# BaseHander, object, image_classifier, image_segementer,
```

```
# object_detector, text_classifier
class MyHandler(BaseHandler):
    def __init__(self):
        super().__init__()
        self.transform = transforms.Compose([
            transforms.Resize(256),
            transforms. CenterCrop(224),
            transforms.ToTensor(),
            transforms.Normalize(mean=[0.485, 0.456, 0.406],
                                 std=[0.229, 0.224, 0.225])
        ])


    # usually do not need to overload this
    """
    def initialize(self, context):
        #Initialize model. This will be called during model loading time
        #:param context: Initial context contains model server system properties.
        #:return:
        self._context = context
        self.initialized = True
        #  load the model, refer 'custom handler class' above for details
        ...
        """

    def preprocess_one_req(self, req):
        """
        Process one single image.
        """
        # get image from the request
        image = req.get("data")
        if image is None:
            image = req.get("body")
         # create a stream from the encoded image
        image = Image.open(io.BytesIO(image))
        image = self.transform(image)
        # add batch dim
        image = image.unsqueeze(0)
        return image

    def preprocess(self, data):
        """
```

```
        Transform raw input into model input data.
        :param batch: list of raw requests, should match batch size
        :return: list of preprocessed model input data
        Process all the images from the requests and batch them in a Tensor.
        """
        requests = data
        images = [self.preprocess_one_req(req) for req in requests]
        images = torch.cat(images)
        return images

    def inference(self, model_input):
        """
        Given the data from .preprocess, perform inference using the model.
        We return the predicted label for each image.
        """
        outs = self.model.forward(model_input)
        probs = F.softmax(outs, dim=1)
        preds = torch.argmax(probs, dim=1)
        return preds

    def postprocess(self, inference_output):
        """
        Return inference result.
        :param inference_output: list of inference output
        :return: list of predict results
        """
        res = []
        # inference_output  [BATCH_SIZE, 1]
        # convert it to list
        preds = inference_output.cpu().tolist()
        # index_to_name.json will be loaded
        # and automatically accessible as self.mapping
        # print(self.mapping)
        for pred in preds:
            label = self.mapping[str(pred)]
            res.append({'label' : label, 'index': pred })
        return res

    # usually do not need to overload this
    """
    def handle(self, data, context):
        #Invoke by TorchServe for prediction request.
```

```
        #Do pre-processing of data, prediction using model and postprocessing of ↩
            prediction output
        #:param data: Input data for prediction
        #:param context: Initial context contains model server system properties.
        #:return: prediction output
        model_input = self.preprocess(data)
        model_output = self.inference(model_input)
        return self.postprocess(model_output)
    """

_service = MyHandler()

# module level entry point
def handle(data, context):
    if not _service.initialized:
        _service.initialize(context)

    if data is None:
        return None

    return _service.handle(data, context)
```

I hope you do not have any trouble understanding it.

More relevant reference documents are: https://pytorch.org/serve/custom_service.html
https://github.com/pytorch/serve/blob/master/docs/custom_service.md
https://github.com/FrancescoSaverioZuppichini/torchserve-tryout
https://github.com/pytorch/serve/blob/master/docs/custom_service.md

Now let's put the custom_handler into a .mar file

```
model-server@d1909dbe9592 $ torch-model-archiver --model-name mydensenet161 \
--version 1.0 \
--model-file ./model.py  --serialized-file ./densenet161-8d451a50.pth  \
--export-path ./model-store --extra-files ./index_to_name.json \
--handler ./custom_handler.py -f
```

Test our custom_handler at:

```
$ curl http://127.0.0.1:8080/predictions/mydensenet161 -T kitten.jpg
{
  "label": "tiger_cat",
  "index": 282
}
```

Yah, it is working!

10.2.4 Management model at runtime

Another great thing about TorchServe is: it provides a set of API allow user to manage models at runtime, that is great.

Again an example is better than a thousand words.

Please read through:

```
# start torchserve without loading any model
$ docker run --rm -it -v $(pwd)/model-store:/home/model-server/model-store \
-p 8080:8080 -p 8081:8081 pytorch/torchserve torchserve --start --ncs \
--model-store model-store

# we verify it:
$ curl http://127.0.0.1:8080/predictions/mydensenet161 -T kitten.jpg
{
  "code": 404,
  "type": "ModelNotFoundException",
  "message": "Model not found: mydensenet161"
}

# Let's check what models did we load?
$ curl "http://localhost:8081/models"
{
  "models": []
}

# now let's add model
# note: the mydensenet161.mar should be accessible from
# model-store within the container
```

```
# or we can also pass a real URI using the HTTP(s) protocol.
# TorchServe can download .mar files from the Internet.
#$ curl -X POST "http://localhost:8081/models?url=http://server/mydensenet161.mar ↩
    "
$ curl -X POST "http://localhost:8081/models?url=mydensenet161.mar"
{
  "status": "Model \"mydensenet161\" Version: 1.0 registered with 0 initial  ↩
      workers.
   Use scale workers API to add workers for the model."
}

# now let's check it
$ curl "http://localhost:8081/models"
{
  "models": [
    {
      "modelName": "mydensenet161",
      "modelUrl": "mydensenet161.mar"
    }
  ]
}

# let's testing
$ curl http://192.168.86.107:8080/predictions/mydensenet161 -T kitten.jpg
{
  "code": 503,
  "type": "ServiceUnavailableException",
  "message": "Model \"mydensenet161\" has no worker to serve inference request.
   Please use scale workers API to add workers."
}

# still not working, but it said we have to add workers
# now use management API to add worker for that model
$ curl -v -X PUT "http://localhost:8081/models/mydensenet161?min_worker=2"
{
  "status": "Processing worker updates..."
}
* Connection #0 to host localhost left intact

# check it
$ curl "http://localhost:8081/models/mydensenet161"
[
```

```
  {
    "modelName": "mydensenet161",
    "modelVersion": "1.0",
    "modelUrl": "mydensenet161.mar",
    "runtime": "python",
    "minWorkers": 2,
    "maxWorkers": 2,
    "batchSize": 1,
    "maxBatchDelay": 100,
    "loadedAtStartup": false,
    "workers": [
      {
        "id": "9000",
        "startTime": "2020-09-21T03:39:16.000Z",
        "status": "READY",
        "gpu": false,
        "memoryUsage": 0
      },
      {
        "id": "9001",
        "startTime": "2020-09-21T03:39:16.010Z",
        "status": "READY",
        "gpu": false,
        "memoryUsage": 0
      }
    ]
  }
]

# now test it
$ curl http://192.168.86.107:8080/predictions/mydensenet161 -T kitten.jpg
{
  "label": "tiger_cat",
  "index": 282
}
```

Hope you get the idea how it works.

More documents at:
https://pytorch.org/serve/management_api.html
https://aws.amazon.com/blogs/machine-learning/
deploying-pytorch-models-for-inference-at-scale-using-torchserve/

10.3 Other integration methods

Pytorch provides a C+\+ frontend. It is a pure C `interface to the PyTorch machine-learning framework, and enables C` programs to directly interface with pytorch's underlying C++ codebase.

Pytorch provides an excellent tutorial at:
https://pytorch.org/tutorials/advanced/cpp_frontend.html

10.4 Summary

After reading this chapter, you should be able to:

- wrap your deep learning model as a REST API service
- deploy your model using TorchServe

Chapter 11

Index

About the author

Benjamin Young is the owner of www.comrite.com, an information technology consulting firm based in Austin, TX, specialized in software development (machine/deep learning, voip, web development etc). He has more than 20 years experience in software engineering, system/network administration.

He can be reached at: benjamin@comrite.com

Or by visiting:

http://amazon.com/author/benjaminyoung

https://github.com/mingewang/

AND PLEASE ...

If you find this book useful, I'd really appreciate a review (no matter how short) on amazon:

Vol. 1: https://www.amazon.com/gp/product/B08JKQLB8Z

Vol. 2: https://www.amazon.com/gp/product/B08JKPS7N5

This will help me continue to write quality books.

Other books by Benjamin Young:

- Deep Learning with Keras from Scratch:
  https://www.amazon.com/gp/product/1091838828/
- Docker for Dummies in Real World:
  https://www.amazon.com/dp/B06Y295S49/

- Kubernetes Quick Start:
  https://www.amazon.com/dp/B08HQTM57N/

www.ingramcontent.com/pod-product-compliance
Lightning Source LLC
LaVergne TN
LVHW081339050326
832903LV00024B/1216

* 9 7 9 8 6 8 8 2 2 3 9 9 6 *